The Consequences of Information

To Marina

For showing me the other side

The Consequences of Information

Institutional Implications of Technological Change

Jannis Kallinikos

London School of Economics, UK

Edward Elgar
Cheltenham, UK • Northampton, MA, USA

Published by
Edward Elgar Publishing Limited
Glensanda House
Montpellier Parade
Cheltenham
Glos GL50 1UA
UK

Edward Elgar Publishing, Inc.
William Pratt House
9 Dewey Court
Northampton
Massachusetts 01060
USA

A catalogue record for this book
is available from the British Library

Library of Congress Cataloging in Publication Data

Kallinikos, Jannis.
   The consequences of information : institutional implications of
technological change / by Jannis Kallinikos.
      p. cm.
   Includes bibliographical references and index.
   1. Information technology—Management. 2. Business enterprises—
Computer networks. I. Title.
   HD30.2.K353 2006
   303.48´33—dc22   2006014313

ISBN-13: 978 1 84542 328 5 (cased)
ISBN-10: 1 84542 328 3 (cased)

Typeset by Cambrian Typesetters, Camberley, Surrey
Printed and bound in Great Britain by MPG Books Ltd, Bodmin, Cornwall

Contents

Figures and tables

Figures

Tables

The technology of information has loosed a profusion of signs and there is by now a rising sense of alarm about the flood of information that, instead of irrigating culture, threatens to ravage it ... Information is about to overflow and suffocate reality.

Albert Borgmann
Holding On to Reality:
The Nature of Information at the Turn of the Millennium

Acknowledgements

Many people have helped me make the ideas of this book better and more coherent. I have over the years retained close contact with my colleagues Hans Hasselbladh (Swedish Institute for Working Life) and Ioanna Tsivacou (Panteion University, Athens) despite the geographical distance separating us. I have greatly benefited from working with each of them on many occasions, sharing ideas orally, and through email or phone conversations. From the two different corners of Europe in which they work and live, Hans and Ioanna have read and commented on extended parts of this book and I am greatly indebted to them for numerable comments and recommendations they have delivered to me.

I would like to extend my appreciation to many of my colleagues at the Department of Information Systems at the London School of Economics and Political Science (LSE) for helping me make my ideas socially relevant, coherent and accessible. I am particularly indebted to Chrisanthi Avgerou, Mike Cushman, Carsten Sorensen and Edgar Whitley for reading and commenting on earlier drafts of the manuscript that became this book. Over the last four years, I have been in charge of the PhD programme of the Department of Information Systems at the LSE. I have thus been in close contact with the PhD students of the Department and benefited greatly from sharing my ideas with them. As a result of trying to help them cope with the variety of conceptual and methodological issues which the writing of the PhD thesis always raises, I came into contact with a variety of exciting research projects that widened my intellectual horizons. I would like specifically to single out and thank Dionysios Demetis, Alexander Grous, Federico Iannacci and Matthew Smith for helping me make this book better both in terms of content and style.

I have also been greatly indebted to Claudio Ciborra for the support and encouragement he provided me during the three years we worked together at the LSE. Unfortunately, Claudio did not live to see the publication of this book, whose central ideas originated in a project on risk and information infrastructures which he led together with Ole Hanseth (University of Oslo) and in which I participated. My discussions with him over the nature of information and communications technologies and the distinctive forms in which they are involved in the making of contemporary economic and social life have always been a source of inspiration. I would like in this context to take the opportunity to thank Ole Hanseth, in whose company I have learnt much about the character of current technological developments and other matters. I would like further to extend my appreciation to Giovan Francesco Lanzara (University of Bologna), with whom I have been able to work closely on several occasions over the last two or three years. Indeed the first version of the Luhmann-inspired theory of technology as functional simplification and closure that permeates this book was first presented in a seminar at the University of Bologna.

I would finally like to thank my friend Nicos Mantousis, with whom I have spent innumerable afternoons and evenings discussing one or other aspect of modern life, reciting and commenting on Bauman, Baudrillard, Borges, Calvino, Kondylis and others. In the yard of his home on the outskirts of my home town, Preveza in western Greece, facing the blue expanses of the Ionian Sea, ideas have often taken another shape and words gained an elegant pattern. Some of these ideas and expressions found their way into this book.

1. Organizations, Information, Networks

1.1 Preamble

For nearly three decades, the organizational arrangements that have accommodated the production of goods and services in the contemporary world have been undergoing significant transformations. The nature, let alone the causes, of these changes remain the object of lively academic controversy (Webster 2002; Yates and Van Maanen 2001). It is, however, customary, since the publication of Daniel Bell's (1976) much-quoted work, to contrast these developments to the stable organizational patterns that underlay the prevailing order of industrialism and modernity. The paradigm of mass production, and the associated efficiency-promoting organizational machinery, have both been in steady decline for the last few decades (Harvey 1989; Piore and Sabel 1984; Storper 1989). At the same time, new modes of work and employment have gradually evolved, calling into question core institutional arrangements (such as the standard employment contract and labour law) defining the forms of individual involvement in formal organizations (Beck 1992, 2000; Marchington *et al.* 2005; Rifkin 1995). These trends have been reinforced by the growing instrumental significance of knowledge and information management and, combined with wider economic and sociocultural changes, have challenged the organizational practices and configurations that prevailed in modern society for a century (Castells 1996, 2000, 2001; DiMaggio 2001; Fukuyama 1997; Zuboff 1988; Zuboff and Maxmin 2003).

The comprehensive character of these developments suggests that the forces that drive these ongoing organizational changes stem from significant shifts at the core of the modern social project and its production apparatus (Harvey 1989; Webster 2002). In this volume, I propose to deal with a somewhat narrower set of issues that explore the relationship between, on the one hand, current organizational transformations and, on the other hand, the rising instrumental significance which techno-logical information has been acquiring over the last few decades. The spectacular diffusion of information, consequent upon the comprehensive organizational and economic involvement of information and communication technologies, is an unquestion-able development, even though its implications are not yet fully understood. Technological information is surely involved in redefining a substantial part of organizational operations, in the sense of steadily reshaping the ends (products and services) and the means (work and managerial processes) through which these ends are achieved. However, the organizational implica-tions of information diffusion reach, I suggest, much further than that.

As technological information penetrates deeper and deeper into the texture of organizational operations, it renders them as computational objects. This is an evasive claim which I dedicate considerable space to analysing and substantiating throughout this volume. It suffices here to note that computation constitutes a substantial part of the task infrastructure of organizations as software code. In so doing it tends to render them transferable across settings or functions and recombinable in ways that allow new fields of action and establish new architectures of control and communication (Kallinikos 1996, 1999; Lilley *et al.* 2004; Zuboff 1988). The diffusion of technological information has often been claimed to lead to the virtualization of reality and the advent of organizational arrangements (virtual organizations) that seek to accommodate this state of affairs. The implications of computation, as I use this term, differ. Computation does not simply transpose reality to an electronic medium. Rather, the inescapable analytic predilection of computation is involved in the far-reaching decomposition of reality and its reconstitution as machine-run code. Apparently simple computer-based appli-cations such as computer-enabled writing are made possible and constructed by the elaborate segmentation of what constitutes writing (or so it is assumed), far beyond the level of observable regularities that handwriting has normally entailed. In this sense, computation reorganizes the universe and reshapes the substratum upon which a substantial part of contemporary modes of action and communication are based (Flusser 2000, 2003).

Technological information is involved in current organizational transformations in yet another sense. As information diffuses within and across organizations, it tends to shift away from local circumstances the perspective from which organizations confront the variety of contingencies that define their operations. In reclaiming the coordination of organizational operations, information steadily introduces considerations and concerns that transcend the functional enclosures of local settings, exposing organizations to forces deriving from a much larger, often global, infospace (such as market, economic or political trends; technological circumstances; and resource and supplier conditions).

The appreciation of the organizational implications of the diffusion of technological information inevitably stumbles over the significance attributed to networks across a multidisciplinary literature (Castells 1996, 2000, 2001; Nohria and Eccles 1992; Powell 1990, 2001; Thompson 2003, 2004). An important part of the volume is therefore dedicated to the critical reappraisal of the claim according to which networks are becoming the key organizational arrangement of the postindustrial age: the operating system, as Castells (2002) envisages it, of the information economy and society. The view that the advent and diffusion of networks question the organizational foundations of the modern industrial order is both appealing and challenging at the same time. On the one hand, it resonates well with a widespread sentiment of change towards flexible, scalable and flatter arrangements that reflect the overall spirit of the age. Against such a background, the term *network* seems to hold a considerable promise not just as an analytical construct but also as a prescriptive tool for organizing the operations of corporations, public agencies and the state (Barry 2001; Castells 2001). On the other hand, the term is analytically opaque and its conceptual value is contingent on whether it can be refined and deployed in ways that step beyond the nebula of significations with which it has been associated.

It would be possible to conjecture that no more than an associative value, heuristic as it were, should be attributed to the term *network*. The term would be viewed as essentially a sensitizing device to the emerging organizational changes.[1] However, the claims which consider networks to be a key transformative

1. I return to this issue later on in this chapter.

agent of the organizational order dominating modernity over the last century must raise a number of profound questions. The scale of the invoked change is of a magnitude demanding a close examination of the organizational arrangements that have dominated the production of goods and services for the last hundred years. The appreciation of the very conditions out of which networks may emerge as a crucial mould of interaction and coordination in the current age makes it necessary to juxtapose them with the organizational arrangements which they are supposed to challenge and the institutions by which these arrangements have been supported. In this process, the close specification of the terms by which networks differ from these arrangements must be spelled out. Oversimplified and stereotyped comparisons – such as networks versus hierarchies – obscure rather than help disclose the distinctive nature of these transformations.

The institutional tangle within which the prevailing organizational arrangements are embedded provides an indication of the complex character of the issues raised by the large-scale change to which networks are commonly tied. Organizational arrangements or forms are never straightforward functional set-ups geared to maximizing output (Fligstein 1990, 2001; Jepperson and Meyer 1991; Scott 1995). They are made possible by, and carried on the shoulders of, solidified social conventions which we recognize as institutions. The institutional order within which organizational arrangements are embedded (property rights, employment contracts, authority systems, distribution of jurisdictions, dominant forms of accountability and so forth) does not simply provide the surrounding normative or legal environment of organizations, but furnishes the very building blocks by which they are constituted as social entities.[2] In other words, formal organizations are institutions or, if one still wants to keep the concepts apart, time-space instantiations of the institutional conditions within which they are embedded (Jepperson and Meyer 1991; Meyer 1994).

It might be possible to conjecture that the detailed consideration of the interpenetration of institutional and organizational arrangements can be bracketed when shorter and less comprehensive organizational change is the major focus of study. In

---

2. It should be clear that functionality as a socially established orientation, principle and set of practices is itself an institution in the meaning attributed to the term by Castoriadis (1987).

such cases, the established institutional order might be taken for granted. Such a choice is, however, not available when large-scale, momentous transformations are considered. With few exceptions (for example, DiMaggio 2001), customary use of the term *network* pays due attention neither to these fundamental issues nor to the ways institutions are implicated in those developments with which networks are supposed to be associated. The appreciation of the significance of networks, therefore, makes necessary the examination of the organizational order of modernity and its foundations. There is no way to capture the organizational shifts underpinning networks without paying due attention to the distinctive qualities of the organizational arrangements of the modern industrial order and the institutions that support them. Crucial to this goal is the juxtaposition of networks with formal organization as a key institutional arrangement of the modern industrial society and the consideration of the regime underlying the constitution of formal organizations as bounded, hierarchically unified and accountable socioeconomic entities. A different picture of current changes emerges out of this juxtaposition that shows the diffusion of networks confronting a thick institutional order with which formal organizations are variously associated. The renegotiation of that order touches upon central principles of the organization of the modern industrial society, such as accountability regimes, employment forms and their ramifying social implications.

The straightforward connection of technological and institutional change that I attempt in this volume runs perhaps counter to a widespread view that stresses the different nature of these two realms, and the distance separating the objectifying and neutral universe of technology from the normative and value-infused world of institutions. However, the degree of the involvement of technological information in contemporary institutional life is comprehensive enough to make that connection plausible and necessary. Two major developments to which I have alluded above can be singled out in this respect. The first of them is associated with the rapid, in some cases exponential growth of information that has been taking place over the last few decades and which has been accelerating since the advent of the internet and the web (for example, Lyman *et al.* 2003). Information growth is a major contemporary development whose far-reaching organizational, social and economic implications are just beginning to be felt. It exhibits strong self-propelling qualities that are associated with the production of information out of available information, a process that is inherently unstable and unpredictable. Growing in this way, information is no longer a resource but a pervading element of socioeconomic life involved in the redefinition of a variety of practices and modes of involvement. An important implication of these developments is the saturation of functional and locally-embedded enclaves with information deriving from a broad infospace constructed by an increasingly interoperable ecology of information and communication technologies. The large and diverse quantities of information invading local contexts steadily expose situated agents to messages, information and requests arriving from distant events or sources and are thus involved in shifting their perspectives away from local concerns. The disembedding qualities of these developments may have a thick tail (Granovetter 1985; Sassen 2001) but they nonetheless participate in establishing new architectures of cognition, action and control that warrant serious consideration.

Less evident and much more elusive are the implications associated with what, in this volume, I shall refer to as the computational rendition of reality. The nature of coding and computationally produced information are such that they make indispensable the relentless and meticulous parsing of reality and its reconstruction as large, often huge, series of automated operations. In this sense, the technological paradigm of computation pierces deep down to the invisible, microscopic texture of things, which it reconstitutes as a large array of computational rules and procedures. In so doing, it exposes (or projects) a new, non-observable realm of reality that can be reconstructed, manipulated and acted upon through software-based representations (Flusser 2000, 2003). Users of information are in contact only with a very limited surface manifestation (the user interface) of this complex, underground as it were, technological edifice. The computational rendition of reality has far-reaching implications in the sense of recapturing a growing proportion of the physical and cognitive landscape of contemporary life into the medium of permutable and recombinable information.[3] A

---

3. So-called Body Area Networks will soon be commercially available to monitor in detail the physiology of our bodies through sensors reporting for instance to mobile phones or other widely diffused electronic devices; see Williams (2006).

key organizational and economic implication of this computational conquest of the microscopic and invisible texture of reality is the dissolvable or decomposable character of many organizational tasks and operations, and the possibilities that are thus emerging for modularizing, packaging and transferring (outsourcing) them across settings. I connect both the disaggregation of organizations and the diffusion of networks with these developments.

In the rest of this introductory chapter I seek to assemble the picture I have been indicating in a somewhat more detailed, yet still brief, fashion.

1.2 Bounded Systems and Networks

Any attempt to describe in wholesale terms the profile of the organizational arrangements that have prevailed over the last century is destined to involve heroic assumptions that inevitably simplify their heterogeneous, and often ambiguous and agonistic nature. However, it is necessary to spell out the distinctive qualities of these arrangements as a means of appreciating better the nature of the current developments. Two major characteristics have commonly been presented as defining the profile of the organizational forms that have dominated the typical modern industrial order: boundedness and hierarchical constitution (Thompson 1967; Tilly 2001; Zuboff and Maxmin 2003). Both private firms and public agencies have been represented as strictly circumscribed cells of collective effort, hierarchically organized. In units of this sort, command over human and other resources is tied to relatively clear organizational boundaries that safeguard hierarchical control and establish the administrative conditions upon which hierarchy can exercise formal authority and enforce order. Clear membership rules and stable internal relationships provide the context within which expectations are defined and tied to fixed job descriptions and specifications forming the basis of rule-bound behaviour. Formal organizations may have never been as neat as this brief, and inevitably simplified, description tends to suggest (March and Simon 1993; Tilly 2001; Winter and Taylor 2001); nevertheless, boundary maintenance, stability and vertical lines of command form a coherent set of principles and conventions instrumental to the construction of bounded systems and the hierarchical patterns of governance associated with such systems (Mintzberg 1979; Thompson 1967).

A commonly advanced argument that depicts the limits and challenges facing these standard structural and administrative arrangements can be roughly sketched as follows. The dominance of formal organizations as bounded and structurally solid entities has been predicated on a stable set of organizational relations. Stability has been afforded and constructed through the relative insulation of organizational operations from environmental contingencies. Organizational closure takes various forms but has mainly been expressed by the standardization of output that provides the point of departure for the standardization of work processes and the technological infrastructure that is deployed in the production of goods and services. The standardization of work processes, and the technological infrastructure, in turn feeds back into the standardization of output. Each reinforces the other in iterative, recursive cycles that make standardization a major strategy of control and efficiency. Environmental change and variation have thus been trivialized and made largely irrelevant to everyday operations. They have been customarily dealt with only periodically (Lampel and Mintzberg 1996), through shifts in products and services and incremental adjustments in structure and strategy (Chandler 1977; March and Simon 1993; Thompson 1967). Overall, responsiveness to environmental variation has been kept at a minimum and has generally been subordinated to the goal of running the core processes of the organizational system as efficiently as possible.[4]

These conditions are believed to have changed dramatically over the last three decades or so. Due to wider economic, technological and sociocultural developments, the construction of the stable relations on which organizational closure had been

4.   Lampel and Mintzberg provide evidence of the drastic reduction in the variety of many industrial goods that occurred during the first half of the twentieth century as the model of mass production gained dominance. 'By 1929, a survey of eighty-four product classes showed a reduction in variety at times amounting to 98 percent of its 1921 level. For example, the number of bed blanket sizes dropped from seventy-eight to twelve; hospital beds that had come in thirty-three sizes were all standardized to a single size by 1929; and the colors of men's hats were reduced from 100 to nine. The vigor of the standardization movement was so pronounced that two French travellers of the period concluded that the U.S. businessman "has standardized the individual in order to standardize manufacture", a claim that they would hardly withdraw today after a visit to McDonald's (Lampel and Mintzberg 1996: 23).

predicated now proves impossible, and most of the time irrelevant or even detrimental. The heterogeneous and largely unpredictable character of the habitat within which most organizations currently operate combines with the fragmentation and eventual individualization of lifestyles and consumption patterns (Bauman 2000; Harvey 1989; Webster 2002) to redefine the established ways by which organizations have traditionally dealt with externally induced change (see for example, DiMaggio 2001; Zuboff and Maxmin 2003). Periodic readjustments will no longer suffice. A radically different organizational relationship to these wider economic, social and cultural trends is deemed necessary. Novel structural configurations are assumed to develop that seek to accommodate environmental change and fragmentation in a genuine and continuous fashion.

In Castells's (1996, 2000, 2001) widely acclaimed account, a new form of economic organization, the network enterprise, emerges both as the epitome of a wide range of social and economic changes and as a vehicle that drives the current transition from the industrial to the informational economy. Castells suggests that the crucial economic role of knowledge combines with the communicative density and the volatile environment of late capitalism to make the gathering, processing, exchange and use of information the axial principle of value creation. Thus, the capacity to respond to the demands imposed by such an axial principle becomes the crucial factor in organizing manpower and resources, and managing organizations. The older structural moulds that have accommodated the production of goods and services are, in this respect, too restrictive. Skills and competences have to be transferred across settings and often reconfigured; messages and information exchanged in interactive patterns; and resources deployed in scalable forms. These practices defy the territorial bounds of organizations, the functional segmentation of their operations and the cumbersome communication patterns associated with the vertical line of command. From this point of view, the quest for alternative economic and organizational practices combines with the impressive instrumental involvement of information and communication technologies to establish the conditions out of which networks emerge as the key structural configuration of the current age.

The developments described above predominantly echo the conditions assumed to underlie the sphere of economy and the operations of private firms. However, similar trends have followed in the public sector and led, over the last two decades, to a considerable restructuring of public agencies and the state in many developed countries. Either through the exercise of normative pressures (du Gay 2005; Clarke and Newman 1997) or for reasons that may well reflect enduring and long-term shifts in the conditions underlying contemporary society[5] (Fountain 2001; Kallinikos 2006b), the operations of the state and its agencies have assumed structural forms isomorphic with the organizational developments I have described. It is worth noting that this new layout of the operations of the state and public agencies has not been limited to administrative and bureaucratic matters. It has also extended to include the strategies and modes by which the contemporary state and some of its agencies safeguard their boundaries, both with respect to the other spheres of the society (such as the economy, science and education) and internationally (Barry 2001; Jessop 2002; Tilly 2001).

1.3   Conceptual Issues

So adumbrated, the picture asserting the rising significance of networks may be hard to question: it appeals to common sense. It is also concordant, as already indicated, with a widespread sentiment and discourse, suggesting changes along similar lines in the modes by which firms and organizations are currently operating, which can be found in managerial and business circles, in the mass media and in parts of academia (see for example Courpasson and Reed 2004; DiMaggio 2001; Malone 2004; Malone and Laubacher 1998). The relevant developments are, furthermore, supported by some empirical evidence, including the spread of outsourcing or downsizing, that has been taken as indicative of the disaggregation of organizations and the creation of independent units which spring out of the disaggregating trends of large, bounded and hierarchical systems (Powell 2001). However, systematic empirical data that would allow the global, albeit not necessarily conclusive, judgement on

5. Some of these factors include, on the one hand, sociopolitical changes like those represented by growing individualization and globalization and, on the other hand, techno-social developments manifested in the key role that information, and the technologies by which it is supported, play in the instrumentation and control of economic and organizational processes. I revisit these issues in Chapters 3, 5, 6 and 7.

whether networks are replacing bounded organizations as the key organizational arrangement in modern times is as yet lacking (DiMaggio 2001). Indeed, the stability of average business size over the last two decades (Kelly 1998) and the continuance of corporate empire building, mergers and acquisitions in some industries of global reach suggest a far more complicated picture of recent developments than the discourse of networks and disaggregation presumes (Brown and Duguid 2000; Harrison 1994; Sassen 2001).

Despite the doubts one might maintain as to the precise character of current developments, it would seem difficult to deny the gradual formation of a new instrumental habitat that differs from those economic, social and organizational conditions that supported concentration and the bounded and hierarchical form of organization. The new electronic forms of communication and data manipulation, and a variety of changes they have brought about, figure among the key characteristics underlying this emerging habitat. Of particular importance has been the high degree of resource mobility which the comprehensive and continuously expanding informatization has conferred upon the broad range of services and organizational tasks that have been so transformed. The rendition of a variety of services and operations as information, mentioned earlier, has enabled their repackaging into discrete information modules that can be lifted out of particular contexts, reshuffled and recombined on a global scale (Mowshowitz 2002; Sassen 2001). Coupled with new modes of communication and action at a distance, informatization has provided both the means and the impetus for trying out alternative forms of cooperation and economic organization.

Are networks the inevitable outcome of these developments? How do the old and the new bear upon one another? In which sense do networks differ from bounded, hierarchical organizations? Do these two organizational arrangements challenge or support one another? What sort of institutional relationships and changes do they presuppose? Answering these questions inevitably requires the careful and detailed reconsideration of the organizational foundations of the modern industrial age. The developments currently under way can be appreciated properly only when situated in their wider historical context, and key defining trends can thus be singled out from secondary or less significant phenomena (Garnham 2004; Reed 2005). Placed against such a background, it would have been reasonable to expect that the claims tied to the concept of network as a key form of collective action would have prompted its definition with sufficient precision to permit the systematic comparison of networks with those economic practices and forms (such as formal organizations and markets) which they are assumed to challenge. However, the loose imagery with which the term *network* has, so far, been associated does not seem to serve that purpose well. Albeit evocative, such imagery does not permit the assessment of the validity of claims that portray networks as a dominant form of economic organization in the late capitalism of the information age. In its current usage, the term appears indeed too broad to be useful in this sense. It is often deployed in a scattergun fashion to designate a large variety of phenomena, ranging from major institutional or organizational forms (Castells 2001; DiMaggio 2001), through business or industry practices (Hirsch 2000; Storper 1993) down to alternative ways of conceptualizing shifting social relations that contrast with traditional group and communal patterns of interaction (Fukuyama 1997; Wellman and Haythornthwaite 2002). This leaves the concept of network under-specified and lacking in analytical or even descriptive power.

Table 1.1 gives an indication of the terminological versatility of the term *network*. Far from being exhaustive, the table is indicative of the wide range of social forms, practices or institutions to which the network has been proposed as a possible alternative.

Contemplating the problems associated with such a fuzzy and indiscriminate way of conceiving of networks, DiMaggio (2001: 213), himself a proponent of the idea of networks as emerging forms of organization, wonders 'whether a term as versatile as "network" deserves a place in social science's conceptual armoury'. Though his critique is less wide-ranging than the one I have been outlining, he too thinks that the fruitfulness of the term depends upon its analytical clarity and the precision with which it is deployed to study the phenomena with which it is said to be associated – a clarity and precision that have so far been lacking.

It is often possible to distinguish concepts in terms of their capacity to disclose rather than describe a reality (Habermas 1987). While being evocative in their power to reveal new aspects of the world, reality-disclosing concepts are often imprecise. The network as construct seems to lie halfway between

Table 1.1   Networks as Alternative Forms of Social Interaction

Network concept	Form of social institution or practice it is posited to replace	Selected literature examples
Network	Formal Organization (Hierarchy)	Castells (1996), Nohria and Eccles (1992), Powell (1990, 2001)
Network	State, State Agencies	Castells (2000), Barry (2001)
Networks (Flexible Specialization)	Mass Producing Organizations	Malone (2004), Piore and Sabel (1984), Storper (1989)
Network	Markets	Malone and Laubacher (1998), Rifkin (2000), Powell (1990, 2001)
Network (Subcontracting and Outsourcing)	Agreements, Vertical Integration	Castells (2001), Malone (2004), Storper (1993)
Network	Group	Wellman (1999), Wellman and Haythornthwaite (2002)
Network, Online Communities	Community	Fukuyama (1997), Wellman and Haythornthwaite (2002), Steinmueller (2002)
Distributed Networking	Co-located Work	DeSanctis and Monge (1999), Schmidt and Bannon (1992), Wellman *et al.* (1996)

these two ideal positions, that is, precision versus disclosure. Perhaps, instead of viewing the versatility or vagueness of the term as a problem, it would be possible to consider it as the very symptom of the situation it seeks to illuminate. Rather than reflecting an inherent conceptual ambiguity, the term could be viewed as the admittedly opaque conceptual mirror of a pervasive social change that cuts through a variety of established practices and institutions. The term, as I have already alluded, could thus be seen as indicative of the current age, providing an opportunity to disclose its distinctive spirit manifested in the preference of social agents for changing relationships and temporary arrangements (Bauman 2000; Lyotard 1984). Such a suggestion is not without merit, as it helps shift attention towards the wider socioeconomic and cultural developments that are associated with the transformation of modernity and its institutional order (Beck 1992; Harvey 1989; Sennett 2006; Tilly 2001).[6] Even if the term *network* is found to have no more than an evocative or associative value, it could be regarded as symptomatic of a number of important economic, institutional and technological changes which it may help single out, and, perhaps, study and describe.

Much of the spirit of this volume develops between these two partly incompatible perspectives. Firstly, I seek to improve the analytical edge of the term *network* through the detailed consideration of certain distinctive traits of formal organizations (such as boundary maintenance, hierarchy and rules of accountability) and the standard technological infrastructures by which they have been supported. In so doing, I counterpose networks with the bounded and hierarchical organization along a number of dimensions, and analyse the ways in which the technological paradigms of industrial and computational technology are implicated in the corresponding organizational arrangements. It is crucial to analyse the distinctive forms through which computation breaks with what I call the instrumental enclosures which industrial technology has constructed and, in so doing, promotes a different task infrastructure upon which new organizational arrangements can emerge. However, shifts in the inherited administrative and structural templates do not equate to institutional change. The bounded and hierarchical organization is not simply an organizational arrangement but is also a central institution of modernity, closely associated with the key modern values of universality, impersonal treatment and accountability

6.	Which position (ethical or ideological) one takes vis-à-vis these changes is another issue.

(see du Gay 2005). Therefore, a fuller appreciation of the issues involved makes it necessary to define the term *network* more precisely and, in this process, to separate the conception of networks as organizational arrangements from that of formal organizations as institutions.

Secondly, I make an effort not to lose sight of the rich associative and heuristic value of the term *network* that ties these organizational arrangements to the wider context of modernity's remaking. Placed against such a backdrop, networks could be seen as a surface manifestation of a much more profound and comprehensive social and economic change. I connect some of these wider socioeconomic changes to the growing involvement of technological information in organizational and institutional life. I draw particular attention to two major, albeit evasive sets of implications of technological informatization that I mentioned in the introductory section to this chapter. The first set is associated with the ever-increasing dissolvability of the fabric of operations that have underlain the production of goods and services. The construction of a pliable organizational reality, coinciding with the dissolvable character of organizational operations, is the outcome of the meticulous and relentlessly analytical decomposition of tasks and processes which formal codification, programming and ultimately informatization bring about. These implications take place at an elementary, microscopic level that often evades empirical observability and must, as a rule, be retraced analytically. The second set of implications develops at the opposite end of these microscopic trends, being related to the disembeddedness that informatization brings about. Information travelling through the extended zones of contemporary interoperable technologies increasingly impregnates particular settings, frames their concerns and remakes their operations (Kallinikos 1996). Strange as it may seem at first glance, dissolvability and disembeddedness are closely associated with and reinforce one another. The very mobility and transference of decontextualized and standardized information are ultimately contingent on informatization's ability to unearth and recapture the minute fabric of many organizational operations and formalize them in information packages.

Placed against the backdrop of the broader system of technological and organizational issues with which it deals, the present volume is not about networks *per se*. It is rather about the transformation of the organizational order of modernity, and the technological changes underlying such a transformation to which, I argue, networks seem to be a central element.

1.4   Themes and Book Structure

In what follows I identify and briefly describe the three major conceptual blocks that make up the argument I put forth and indicate how these are distributed over the various chapters of this volume.

Networks and Technology

Networks have been variously, but constantly, associated with the rising significance of information and the computational/ transactional infrastructure that computer-based technologies provide. However, contemporary social theory, I claim, does not have at its disposal an adequate account of how technology has been implicated in the making of those bounded, circumscribed cells of economic activity that dominated the production of goods and services in industrial capitalism (Kallinikos 2005). There is a general understanding of the factory system, and the organizational arrangements it subsequently occasioned, as being closely associated with the material constitution of industrial technology and its concomitant strong geographical or site dependence (Chandler 1977; Winter and Taylor 2001). But with few exceptions (for example, Luhmann 1993; Zuboff 1988), the relevant literature exhibits a remarkable lack of analytically detailed accounts of how the distinctive nature of industrial technology and the instrumental enclosures it has produced are associated with the bounded and hierarchical character of the dominant organizational arrangements (Kallinikos 2005).

The lack of an adequate treatment of these matters becomes particularly evident when set against an understanding of networks as closely associated with computer-based infrastructures. The rejection of a simple, unequivocal causality that traces organizational arrangements back to technical characteristics does not exempt us from studying the organizational and institutional implications which major technological paradigms may have. It would indeed seem strange to assume that the pervasive involvement of technology in institutional life, so characteristic of the contemporary world, is devoid of implications or that these implications are of no significance. And yet, social theory has for several reasons regarded technology from a distance. While there has been a general and widespread understanding of modernity as a technological society (for example, Giddens 1990), the detailed analytical study of the social and institutional implications of technological change have seldom been seriously pursued (Misa *et al.* 2003) outside the realm of philosophy (Borgmann 1984, 1999; Ellul 1964; Winner 1977, 1986).[7] Given this state of affairs, I believe it necessary to articulate an analytical account of technology that discloses those characteristics (concentration versus dispersion, materiality versus computation) which distinguish the two paradigms of industrial versus information and communication technology.[8]

There are of course some challenging problems that must be addressed as a means of dealing with the cardinal issues of how technology is implicated in the making of social and institutional forms. The transactional nature of technology must be identified and distinguished from the configuration of social interactions to which it may be associated. In turn, technology and social interaction must be distinguished from the organizational arrangements and the institutions supporting them. In other words, technology, the interactive order, the structural order and the institutional order must be kept analytically distinct (Knorr-Cetina and Bruegger 2002). At the same time, their mutual implication and the ways they reinforce one another must be worked out. As a complex, enduring system composed of a large series of objectifying strategies superimposed upon one another, technology is a

7. I do not mean context-embedded studies of particular technologies of the type which Actor-Network Theory (Law 1991) or Science and Technology Studies (Bijker *et al.* 1987; Bijker 2001) and situated approaches (Orlikowski 2000; Suchman 1996) exemplify and which abound. I have more in mind the historical study of technology and its context-free understanding as a major regulative regime that can be associated with major shifts in social practices and institutions, a project that contrasts sharply with the agenda of ANT and STS and their unspoken but clear interactionist legacy. See the next two chapters, and Luhmann (1993) and Kallinikos (2004c, 2005). For a thorough criticism of ANT and STS and their intellectual roots see Klaus (2004).
8. Such a project must be distinctively different too from descriptive historical studies that deal with the emergence of large centralized systems and the historical antecedents of information technology (for example, Chandler 1977; Chandler and Cortada 2000; Forester 1989; Yates 1989) even though it will draw from the empirical wealth such studies often provide.

potent agent of social and institutional change and the ways it is implicated in such change must accordingly be analysed and appreciated. In the next chapter (and in some respects throughout this volume), I deal with some of these questions in an effort to show how organizational arrangements are associated with the distinctive characteristics of the paradigms of industrial and computational technologies. In so doing I trace back the emerging significance of networks to the centrality which computational information processing and exchange increasingly assume both as a means and an end product of organizational operations.

Computation and Information Growth

The fuller appreciation of the organizational and institutional implications of the computational paradigm makes necessary the detailed analysis of the distinctive ways by which information is implicated in the remaking of the instrumental landscape of the contemporary world. There is a huge literature on this subject which I shall draw on. There are two significant issues, though, that have not been given the required attention and which must, therefore, be explored further. The first, which I referred to above, concerns the far-reaching effects information processing has for dissolving (and not simply dematerializing or virtualizing) the compact, *en bloc* character of tasks and operations that become informatized and in this way contributing to reconstituting them as manipulable code and lifting them out of their context embeddedness. The transformation of the thick texture of organizational operations that are by necessity heavily embedded in local contexts to a dissolvable, informatized and module-made ensemble of processes and services is opening a new realm of enlarged resource mobility, transferability and combinability, of which financial services stand as the exemplar. These characteristics in turn establish a set of technical conditions on the basis of which humans and resources can be constantly reshuffled and reassembled on a global scale, thus leading eventually to the emergence and diffusion of new modes of social and economic organization (Mowshowitz 2002; Sassen 2001).

However, the hypermobility of resources, services and operations makes it necessary for us to understand not simply informatization but crucially the very dynamics of information growth, and the forms through which information penetrates every walk of social, organizational and institutional life. The explosive growth of information by necessity leads to the infor-matized rendition of reality on a massive scale. Technically-mediated representation reconstitutes, stands for, frames and controls a significant proportion of institutional processes. This marks a significant shift that makes technological information the generalized currency, as it were, of most institutional and social life. The continuing dynamic of information growth is a highly complex and systemically reproduced phenomenon that cannot adequately be analysed in terms of agency-centric expla-nations that assign methodological priority to the objectives, interests and strategies of social agents. Rather, such a dynamic is, to a significant degree, a self-propelling and partially uncon-trollable process that represents one of the distinctive character-istics of the current age. Thus, it must be analysed on its own and its far-reaching social, organizational and institutional implica-tions assessed. I take up these issues in Chapters 3 and 4 and, to a certain degree, in Chapter 5. In Chapter 4 I further consider some central and highly controversial issues concerning the role which agency and meaning assume in the current dynamics of information growth. The chapter is indeed a commentary on the de-centred forms by which agency is implicated in the growth of technological information.

Formal Organizations

Formal organizations, as I have already mentioned, are not simply structural arrangements for the accomplishment of goals and the production of goods and services. Structural and orga-nizational arrangements are instantiations of, or at least expres-sions of, institutions and the codification of social experience and struggles that institutions embody (Fligstein 1990, 2001; Meyer 1994). The bounded, hierarchical organization coincides with what, after Weber (1978), is broadly known as the bureau-cratic form of organization. Bureaucracy has been associated in the popular imagery, and to some degree in the social science disciplines, with a variety of negative attributes. This is unfortu-nate as it has often tended to obscure the degree to which bureaucracy constitutes a fundamental institution of the modern world (Du Gay 2005). Even though the bureaucratic constitution of formal organizations could to a certain extent be understood in functionalist terms as a structural mechanism for dealing with complexity in social settings (coordination) such an understanding is, to say the least, inadequate. Bureaucracy is not simply a 'cell of economic activity' (Castells 2000, 2001) nor just a model for running the operations of firms and organizations. The bureaucratic organization is above all an institutional fold, a rational legal regime of accountable behaviour that has been the outcome of complex cultural and social developments. These reflect, among other things, the institutional embeddedness of property rights and the employment contract and the legal and socio-political processes for assigning jurisdictions and laying out the rules of accountability in democratic societies.

The broad usage of the term *network* is associated with the frequent failure to distinguish clearly the institutional status of organizations and differentiate them from what I referred to above as the interactive and structural orders. The issue is not terminological, though the lack of an established terminology makes things worse. An ensuing consequence of this state of affairs is, I suggest, the substitution of a variety of functional or social arrangements for organizational forms and, frequently, confusion of them. The comparison of networks with bureaucracy, in particular, is predicated on such a category error, counterposing a core institution of the modern industrial order with those patterns of interaction and collaboration which the concept of network seeks to describe. The economic, social and technological developments which are associated with the ongoing restructuring of industrial capitalism may have far-reaching organizational consequences (Castells 2001; DiMaggio 2001; Kumar 1995) but ones that cannot be gauged by this false antithesis. Despite its resonance, such a comparison is misleading. This elision conceals the issues that are at stake and misdirects attention from those factors or processes that account for the developments more convincingly associated with networks. I deal with these questions initially in Chapter 5 and more thoroughly in Chapters 6 and 7.

In the final chapter of this volume I bring together again the three blocks of arguments (networks and technology, computation and information growth and formal organizations) advanced in the other chapters and discuss some of the wider implications of the current technological and institutional developments.

2. Technological Design and Social Systems

2.1 Technology and Organizations

Electronic networks are commonly tied to the information arteries that networked computer-based technologies provide, even though the network as an organizational arrangement involves the transfer not simply of data but crucially also of messages, orders and decisions. The ability to sustain communication and information exchange over the electronic medium is, nonetheless, a necessary condition for developing, across established institutional, organizational and geographical boundaries, the variety of links associated with networks (Castells 1996, 2000, 2001; DeSanctis and Monge 1999; Mowshowitz 2002). Contemporary technologies of information and communication are, though, a potent means of information processing and storage; to appreciate more fully the implications of the growing organizational and economic involvement of these technologies, it is necessary to understand them as more than a connecting medium. Information has to be produced, organized and stored in appropriate forms, before it becomes exchangeable and transferable across contexts.

Information processing and storage currently represent the backbone of many organizational operations. Over the last fifty years or so, computer-based systems have been massively deployed to carry out a variety of computational tasks. In so doing, by accident or design, they have been instrumental in reshaping the administrative processes and managerial practices by which organizational operations have been traditionally planned and controlled (Castells 1996; Kling 1996; Yates and Van Maanen 2001; Zuboff 1988). The widespread involvement of computer-based technologies in organizational and social activities has been a critical factor in rendering the heterogeneous, and for that reason instrumentally refractory, character of physical and cultural reality into a disembodied and pliable universe constructed by technological information (Borgmann 1999). An expanding number of domains of palpable reality are carried, in surrogate forms, on the shoulders of technological informatization that describes, renders or constitutes, controls and monitors different aspects of social and institutional life. In thus making reality pliable and mobile, informatization has been an important precondition for the diffusion of alternative administrative models and work patterns.

The rendition and reconstitution of physical and social reality as information seem a rather straightforward consequence of the massive involvement of information and communication technologies in organizations. Less conspicuous and substantially more evasive is the shift these developments signify in terms of the design and instrumentation of technological processes and the organizational implications ensuing from such a shift. Traditional technological design relies heavily on two fundamental principles that Luhmann (1993) subsumes under the terms *functional simplification* and *closure* (see, also, Kallinikos 2005). I shall deal with these principles in some detail later on in this chapter. It suffices here to say that functional simplification coincides with the identification and selection (hence the reduction of complexity) of sets of operations that are thereby instrumented as strict cause–effect couplings in which a particular cause is expected to lead to its specific effects. The construction and smooth functioning of a thus simplified functional order makes it necessary to seal off the technological sequences, to the highest possible degree, from external influences that may interfere and disturb their firm and recurrent unfolding. This way the technological system admits inputs from its environment along highly selective paths while its interface with humans or other systems becomes strictly regulated.

The construction of instrumental enclosures of this sort has had important organizational implications that are strongly tied to the bounded character of formal organizations. Technology has been brought to bear heavily on the arrangement of throughput processes, furnishing the operative core of organizations on the basis of which work and managerial practices have developed (Mintzberg 1979, 1983; Parsons 1956a, b). Meanwhile, technology, as a sealed-off order, has provided the normative model on the basis of which organizations have been constituted as boundary-maintaining, strictly circumscribed systems (Parsons 1956a, b; Scott 1981; Thompson 1967). Contemporary technological developments are widely assumed to question the logic of these control strategies (Castells 1996, 2001). Connectivity and the largely inter-operable character of the tasks or processes made possible by technological informatization challenge, at least in some respects, the stable boundaries which traditional strategies of technological control have been able to establish. Yet the proper understanding of this challenge necessitates a detailed analysis of traditional strategies of technological control and the exposition of the distinctive ways by which the paradigm of information and communication technologies reinforces or modifies these strategies (Kittler 1997). This constitutes an important analytic project that has seldom been pursued in a systematic fashion.

In the rest of this chapter I take up these issues. I initially consider the implications that seem to be associated with the increasing penetration and control of socially and physically embedded processes by technologically-constructed information. I subsume the relevant issues under the heading of 'the disembeddedness of labour and administration' to provide an important focus for the present chapter and also to suggest at least some continuity with those processes industrial capitalism once inaugurated. I subsequently move on to describe technology as a bounded order, laying out in some detail the principles of functional simplification and closure and the ways in which the instrumental enclosures which these principles help construct are associated with the bounded and hierarchical organization. In connection with that, and contrary to widely-held views, I initially consider the ways in which computer-based automation and standardization in some respects reinforce, rather than weaken, the key orientation of industrial technology which is manifested in the construction of instrumental enclosures. I then venture into an exploration of the distinctive nature of computation as a technological paradigm, trying to depict why and how it reframes the standard strategies of technological control epitomized by functional simplification and closure. Along the way I develop arguments regarding the organizational implications associated with the two major technological paradigms of industrial versus information and communication technology.

2.2 Disembeddedness: Labour and Administration in Perspective

For over half a century now, computer-based information technologies have been brought to bear on the restructuring of organizational operations through the automation of work processes and the administrative and managerial tasks that are associated with the production and distribution of goods and services. In many respects, such a project could be seen as having carried forward the legacy of the industrial tradition of work transformation and rationalization through technical means (Braverman 1974; Noble 1984; Zuboff 1988).

However, as a technology, computer-based information processing epitomizes an unambiguous cognitive (computational) orientation that strongly differentiates it from the industrial project of reconstructing or duplicating physical processes and human- or animal-based locomotive operations (Simon 1969, 1977). It comes then as no surprise that computer-based technologies have initially been deployed for the rationalization of routine or quasi-routine cognitive tasks (Forester 1989). In this role, they have, to a considerable degree, succeeded and complemented paper-based systems of information processing (archives, indexes, accounting systems) and amended the functionality of the relevant processes in many and interesting ways (Benedikt 1991; Beniger 1986; Zuboff 1988). It is well known that the accuracy and speed of computer-based information processing have vastly improved the performance of computational tasks. Less evident are the effects that have emerged out of the bringing together and juxtaposition of a variety of data and information items that remained unrelated in the old paper-based culture. Most crucially, perhaps, the computational (digital) constitution of computer-based technologies of information has enabled the reconciliation of the incompatibilities intrinsic to traditional media and communications technologies (visual, aural and printing) and the construction of what is referred to as multimedia (Kittler 1996, 1997). As the result of these processes, technological information has become a potent instrument of cognitive perspective and information depth by means of which new and penetrating versions of social reality can be constructed through the comparison and juxtaposition of a large variety of information items and sources (Lilley *et al.* 2004).

At the same time, the gradual overcoming of the technical differences underlying traditionally discrete communication media and their digitally-enabled integration has established an entirely new set of conditions whose instrumental significance still awaits careful analysis. Two implications with far-reaching consequences should, however, be pointed out in this context. The first concerns the separation of interaction from communication historically introduced by writing (Bolter 1991; Ong 1982). By bringing together the various technical media which have separately relied on the decoupling of interaction from communication, computer-based technologies amplify that separation and deepen its social consequences. At the same time, they manage to overcome some of the limitations such a separation has inflicted by reconstituting the bond between interaction and communication at the level of a mediated, technologically-sustained orality (Ong 1982), generating a façade of immediacy. The second implication coincides with the decoupling of the processes of generating information from those of communication, consequent upon the layers of automated rules for information processing which these technologies embody (Kittler 1996, 1997). Together, the separation of interaction from communication and information from communication have had extensive instrumental (and certainly social) implications, some of which I try to analyse later in this chapter and in later chapters.

Communication and, to a certain degree, information were first divorced from interaction on a comprehensive scale through writing. In forming an adequate and historically informed understanding of computer-based technologies of information and communication we must, therefore, not lose sight of the social processes and cognitive habits with which the diffusion of various systems of writing, as distinct from face-to-face interaction, have been associated (Eisenstein 1979; Goody 1977, 1986; Ong 1982). The invention and deployment of various symbol systems and schemes have always been essential for amending the instrumentality of social relations. Physical, and also cultural, reality are heterogeneous and the various compartments they are made of are irreducible one to another. For that reason they remain instrumentally refractory and have to be refashioned at the level of representation on to which physical entities and social relations can be decomposed, recast, rehearsed, mastered and manipulated (Borgmann 1999; Cooper and Kallinikos 1996; Zuboff 1988). Language, representation and specialized systems of writing and notation have all been variously involved in the construction and mediation of the world, and the coordination of human action across space and time (Beniger 1986; Hoskin and Macve 1986; Townley 1994). Computer-based technologies of information and communication continue and simultaneously give new momentum to these processes. The inextricably standardized modes of information processing (data entry standardization, automated

procedures of information processing, data output standardization) and the comprehensive character of the project of informatization participate in the lifting of particular information-
related tasks out of those settings to which they were once
closely tied. Computational descriptions of reality can be transferred and exchanged across contexts, and accessed and manipulated at a distance. The overall outcome of these developments
has been the changing character of labour and administration
along lines that make the tasks and processes by which they are
sustained increasingly disembedded (Mowshowitz 2002; Zuboff
1988).

Computer-based technologies have been deployed in manu-
facturing and other settings of the contemporary society too,
most often as a meta-technology of control, monitoring or
surveillance. Technologically generated information has thus
been used to control and steer the operations of other technologies involved in the transformation or monitoring of physically
embedded processes in industrial plants and in a variety of other
settings of contemporary society, such as the monitoring of free-
way, railway or air traffic (Kallinikos 1999, 2005). In this respect,
contemporary technology has been involved in the refashioning
of the very materiality of traditional modes of work and involvement by transforming the premises of human intervention into
physically-embedded processes (Zuboff 1988). The inescapably
bodily character of industrial work, consequent upon its constitution as physical action aiming at transforming materials, has
progressively given way to the action, manipulation and control
of software-based representations, which have thus become an
indispensable and central element of nearly all contemporary
instrumental engagement (Kallinikos 1996, 1999; Lilley *et al.*
2004; Sotto 1991; Zuboff 1988). Computer-based technologies
have thus given the industrial project of standardizing and
disembedding labour and administration a new and interesting
shift.

Of course, the way these developments have been manifested
varies significantly across industries, organizations and activity
systems. However, the task of reflecting on the social and organizational implications of computer-based technology over
larger time spans raises a number of crucial questions. A key
question concerns whether the instrumental involvement of
computer-based systems exhibits any general features that cut
across the huge variety of settings upon which they have been

brought to bear. Research in information systems, organization studies and, to a large extent, sociology has as a rule been very hesitant in advancing generalizations of this sort (Bijker *et al.* 1987; Bijker 2001; Kling 1966; Orlikowski 2000). Universal rationalism casts long shadows. The danger of oversimplification, loss of nuance and specificity has combined with a deep academic fragmentation to make reflection on the distinctive character of the technological paradigm of information and communication technologies and its implications rare. However, no matter how rich and insightful they might be, situated studies of particular technologies in specific settings provide little guidance to the fundamental issue concerning the organizational implications of computer-based technology over larger time spans and across settings. How are the new technologies of information and communication implicated in those comprehensive socio-economic transformations that we touched upon in the preceding chapter? What sort of claims can be made concerning the role of these technologies in the asserted transition from hierarchical organizations to networks, from bounded, stable systems to transitory assemblages of actors and resources across boundaries?

Placed against a wider historical background, the increasing involvement of computer-based technologies of information and communication has by necessity implied the increasing penetration of local contexts by the abstract requirements and standardized procedures which information packages embody. The comprehensive institutional involvement of writing and the development of traditional technical media and communications technologies have produced a variety of modes of generating, processing and storing information that relied on considerable cognitive standardization (such as classification principles and accounting standards). However, paper-based systems remained as a rule rooted in local practices and have seldom influenced one another (Dreyfus 2001). The relatively recent rendition of information at the level of interoperable computer-based systems has changed this situation and enhanced standardization considerably (Dreyfus 2001; Kittler 1997). The social and organizational implications of these developments may vary across contexts and the exact nature of the changes they bring about may be debatable and even highly controversial (Kling 1996). However, to deny the penetration of local contexts by the standardized character of technologically generated information amounts to turning one's back on reality. Standardization of data items and procedures is, indeed, an essential functional prerequisite for the transfer and exchange of information across contexts and the establishment of practices of networking. Compatible and interoperable information systems rely substantially on the establishment of data exchange protocols, and the extensive standardization of data items and procedures (Hanseth 2000, 2004; Kittler 1996). The implications of these processes cut across the local appropriation of particular systems and technologies and their adaptation to the specific demands of local contexts. Standardized information becomes the functional currency, as it were, by means of which locally-embedded processes are drawn out of their specificity and become measurable, manipulable and exchangeable across a variety of contexts and regulative frameworks.

Technological standardization has, however, been essential to industrial capitalism.[1] The current argument therefore calls for explicating both the similarities and differences of the two tech-

---

1. The technologies and the various systems of work and representation which firms and formal organizations have deployed for the management and control of the labour process in industrial capitalism have been extensively predicated upon the standardization of physical and mental labour. This is a lesson already to be learned from *The Capital* (Marx 1954, 1956) and other major works on technology and contemporary work (including Arendt 1958; Braverman 1974; Noble 1984; Mumford 1934, 1952). What are, then, the differences that the paradigm of information and communication technologies brings about? In industrial capitalism, labour disembeddedness mostly took the form of the steady transformation of concrete labour (use value) into abstract labour (exchange value), coinciding with the production of standardized products – commodities. Despite having been invaded by the typifications of the market (commodities to be exchanged) and the standardization brought about by technology and social organization, labour in industrial settings managed to retain essential elements of its concrete status and a sort of recognizable unity expressed in relatively clear-cut job assignments and identifiable career paths (Beck 1992; Kallinikos 2003). Work in industrial capitalism remained by and large anchored in particular places. The industrial workplace always provided the bounds and the generative matrix by which material, skills and labour (use values) combined to produce commodities (exchange values) to enter the abstract equivalences (prices) of market exchange. This state of affairs seems to be subject to a remarkable shift as digitized, technological information becomes a major productive force. In recapturing work processes and operations as systems of formal codes, contemporary technologies of computing and information seem to deliver the definitive blow to the physical constitution of work (Deleuze 1995; Kallinikos 1999).

nological paradigms in a somewhat elaborate fashion. From a certain point of view, the standardization of information tokens and procedures of information processing may seem relatively innocent, compared to the irreversible and inflexible standardization of hardwired machines and the work processes they have allowed. Little wonder then that contemporary information and communication technologies are often understood as providing much more flexible and locally adaptable (reconfigurable) solutions than has been the rule in industrial systems.

The relevance of this observation must however be evaluated against the kinds of standardization exemplified by each of the two technological paradigms. The cross-contextual transferability of industrial technologies has confronted a powerful limit that has reflected both their physical constitution and, most crucially, the fundamental incompatibility of different industrial technological systems or artefacts. Standardization has remained either local or technology-specific. Industrial technologies can be brought to bear upon one another (such as rail and air traffic) but they never intersect. In operational terms, they remain independent and self-contained systems based on very different technical principles. To some degree the same applies to media and communications technologies prior to digitization. Computer-based technology is different in this respect. Whatever incompatibilities exist in hardware and software, they are in principle resolvable. There are no intrinsic limits as to what may become compatible in software technology, even though the practical difficulties in designing and constructing interoperable systems may be substantial. This potential compatibility is due to the computational, binary nature of computer-based technology and the common code language computation brings about. This is a major claim and I examine this relationship in more detail in section 2.5 of this chapter. Prior to that though, it is necessary to venture an analysis of technology as a bounded order and assess its implications with respect to the organizational arrangements with which such a bounded order is associated.

2.3   Technology as Bounded Order

As I have pointed out earlier, there is a widespread understanding in the literature (DeSanctis and Monge 1999) according to which the shift away from the bounded, hierarchical organization is closely associated with the transition from the industrial

to the new technological paradigm of information and communication technologies. While basically correct, such an assumption has rarely been supported by detailed analytical
argumentation. The association of the two major technological
paradigms with the organizational arrangements of bounded or
hierarchical organizations versus networks has, by and large,
remained vague. Even such a thorough analytical project as that
represented by Castells's major work (1996) does not go far
beyond widely accepted assumptions, whereby information and
communication technologies are largely portrayed as an intelli-
gent system capable of acting upon and manipulating information and knowledge, and as a networking medium. The
practices associated with the instrumental utilization of knowledge and information are assumed to be difficult to accommodate within the old bounded and hierarchical systems and they
thus exercise pressures for new structural moulds and practices
of economic coordination. However, and despite the explicit or
implicit importance attributed to information processing and the
technologies by which it is carried out, the detailed analysis of
the distinctive ways by which they reframe the processes, procedures and structures of control in complex systems has never
been seriously pursued. Strange as it may seem, there are very
few studies addressing the issue concerning the general forms
by which technology (industrial or digital) is implicated in the
making of the premises of control underlying the operations of
complex instrumental systems (Beniger 1986; Luhmann 1993;
Perrow 1967, 1984; Simon 1969).[2] Perhaps the ghost of technological reductionism has steered attention away from the
detailed study of the organizational implications of technologies.

However, an adequate appreciation of current developments
requires the demonstration of the distinctive contribution industrial technology has made in the constitution or regulation of the

2. The issue of the general principles or strategies embodied in technological
    design and their organizational implications is distinct from the structural
    implications of different industrial technologies (craft, mass producing and
    process technologies) that were investigated empirically during the 1960s
    and 1970s. For a summary see Zuboff (1988). Similar studies have since
    been conducted in an effort to depict the mechanization of office work
    consequent upon the standardization and automation brought about by
    mainframe computer systems. For a summary see Forester (1989) and
    Kling (1996).

organizational relations that have dominated capitalism until now. Such a project assumes that, despite its contextual variation, technology is a complex regime of practices and techniques, a technological paradigm, as it were, for organizing the relationship between social, cognitive and material processes: an assumption that I seek to justify below. Before taking up that issue, let me state again that the thorough examination of the organizational implications of technology as a regulative regime represents an essential complement to a 'higher' level institutional analysis of organizational forms. Such an examination is made all the more urgent by the variety of claims made for and against the transformative power of computer-based technologies of information and communication (Kling 1996; Woolgar 2002). For in juxtaposing the control strategies of the two technological paradigms and the ways they reinforce but also depart from one another, it could perhaps become possible to disclose the distinctive contribution they have made in the organizational patterns and relations underlying both bounded social systems and networks.

The claim that institutional or economic relations are associated with distinctive technological traditions attributes technology an important role in the making of institutional reality. Given the strong, and to a certain degree justified, reservations against claims of this sort, it would seem appropriate to deliver some clarifying remarks at this point. Modern science-based technology embodies a distinctive logic, sufficiently demarcated against the logics of other major social spheres such as politics, economy or social structure (Heller 1999). This is a major claim, which I would like to underscore against the background of a widespread and often naïve version of constructivism[3] that has become quite common over the last two decades or so. The conception of technology as a distinctive sphere of the contemporary world does not mean attributing to it an asocial status rooted in a trans-historical nature. Rather, it implies that we cannot adequately understand the origin, dynamics and ramifying implications of technological

---

3. I mean the way constructivism has frequently been practised, not necessarily constructivism *per se*. See Thomas Luckmann's lecture at the London School of Economics and Political Science delivered in February 2005 (http://is2.lse.ac.uk/Events/LuckmannLecture.pdf). For an excellent summary of the issues, traditions and problems associated with constructivism see Hacking (1999).

processes together with the phenomena that are constituted and regulated by recourse to technical means without serious consideration of the ways they presuppose, cause and bear upon one another. Technology has, by now, a sufficiently long developmental trajectory in the course of which a large variety of methods, artefacts and objectifying strategies have been superimposed upon one another to make it a complex and to some degree a self-reinforcing domain. The history of technology and its comprehensive involvement in the regulation of human affairs both render the attempt simply to reduce it to social relations hopelessly parochial (Borgmann 1984, 1999; Heller 1999).

As a major and distinctive modality of social coordination, technology matters predominantly in two ways: as a system with specific functionalities and procedures supplied by particular technologies; and as a general form for regulating social relations. In the former case, technology is understood in productivist or instrumentalist terms. It is basically conceived as a means to higher productivity or enhanced human or social performance in those domains to which it is applied. Such a view is typical among economists and management scholars. In the latter case, technology is seen as a complex regulative regime that participates in the constitution of social and organizational relations along predictable and recurrent paths. As a regulative regime,[4] technology represents a major means for managing and controlling contingencies (Bloomfield and Vurdubakis 2001), a key instrument for 'the taming of chance', to use Hacking's (1990) suggestive words. The management of contingencies obviously has serious implications for performance, but such implications derive from the overall design control principles which technology embodies and from which it can seldom be separated.

As suggested in the introduction to this chapter, traditional technological design embodies its strategies of control in the twin principles of functional simplification and closure (Luhmann 1993: ch. 5). Functional simplification, *funktionierende*

---

4. I collapse here the difference between constitutive and regulative means or rules. Technology does help bring about aspects of the real that would never have been possible without the means it provides yet it does so with the ultimate purpose of control and regulation. In this sense, and for practical purposes, I have understated the difference between constitutive and regulative means here.

Simplifizierung,[5] coincides with the identification of an operational domain, within which the complexity of the world is reduced by being reconstructed as a simplified set of causal or instrumental relations. Simplified, in this context, does not mean simple. Functional simplification refers to the reduction of an initial complexity of a particular domain accomplished by the reduction of the number of variables and interactive sequences involved. Indeed, technological processes can be quite complex in themselves and their causal force significantly magnified – for example nuclear power, process technologies or motorway traffic systems. However, due to the initial reduction of the factors involved, the relevant processes remain potentially inspectable and controllable, while the knowledge that enables them provides an important means for the accomplishment of these goals. Functional closure, on the other hand, implies the construction of a kind of protective cocoon (from fences to social practices) that is placed around the selected causal sequences or processes to safeguard undesired interference and ensure their repeatable and reliable operation. Functional simplification and closure implicate one another and straightforwardly express, Luhmann claims, the *Geist* of technology in modern times as instrumental enclosures. The predictable forms by which technology often (but not always) operates, are precisely due to the construction of simplified or planned causalities. The recurrent unfolding of these chained causal sequences is ensured through the organized exclusion (or the attempt at such an exclusion) of contingent forces that could impinge on and disturb the operation of such a functionally simplified order.

The account of technology as a strictly circumscribed causal order is well captured in the widely used engineering term *blackboxing*. It is also re-encountered across a number of key texts on organizations that thus provide evidence about the key issue of the mutual accommodation and interpenetration of social and technical systems (Mintzberg 1979; Perrow 1986; Thompson 1967). Technological processes in organizations provide a core set of operations that embody particular interactive patterns and causal loops characterized by a significant degree of delimitation or closure vis-à-vis other organizational operations. The interface of

5. The German term alludes to the dynamic character of this process. To translate however literally into English as 'functioning simplification' would have been awkward and perhaps slightly misleading.

technology with its environment – social organization, materials, other technologies – encodes a highly selective set of presuppositions in terms of admissible inputs. That is, both resources and human operations enter the technological system through highly selective paths that are made possible by the prior shaping of resource inputs and the development of skill profiles and learning. By these means, the probability of contingent forces entering the system is lowered and human intervention on technological loops becomes regulated along constructed activity corridors (Introna 1997). Organizations further construct the protective cocoon of technology through extensive reliance on such methods as forecasting, stockpiling, procedural control of inputs and other kinds of buffers (Chandler 1977; Thompson 1967). All these mechanisms and procedures aim to ensure the undisturbed unfolding of technological operations by decoupling them from organizational or wider environmental variation to the highest possible degree (Baecker 2006).

Functional simplification and closure thus produce one of the milestones of the organizational arrangements of the modern age: the decoupling of the operations of the technical system from the wider organizational and social relations within which such a system is embedded. Two major organizational subsystems are thereby established whose interfaces and regulation emerge as the key issue facing organizations (Luhmann 1993; Mintzberg 1979, 1983). In principle, social contact with the cause–effect loops of the technological core is kept at a minimum. When such a contact is deemed necessary it tends to become highly regulated through prescriptions, the specification of skill profiles and requirements and role formation. Thus understood, technology has been centrally involved in the making of the dominant organizational practices and the structural templates – command and hierarchy, role differentiation, procedural reporting – by which these practices have been managed (Perrow 1967, 1984). Key design characteristics of the organizational paradigm of the bounded, hierarchical organization such as the standardization of output and of throughput processes have been accommodated by a technological infrastructure that has critically assumed the form of a quasi-enclosed system. Less conspicuous are the implications of the normative and prescriptive model which technology management has tended to promote. Technology has made domain delimitation, closure and highly selective interaction with its environment the key principles for managing the contingent character that besieges many an operation in the contemporary world (Luhmann 1993, 1995, 1998). In so doing, it has provided an ideal, and in practice successful, model of management by means of functional differentiation, and boundary setting and maintenance (Baecker 2006; Introna 1997).

2.4 Computation as Bounded Order

The understanding of technology predicated on the principles of functional simplification and closure derives from industrial experience and the character of industrial technology as predominantly a system for dealing with the management and transformation of materially-based processes. Computer-based technology differs in this respect. Rather than dealing with material processes or impacts, it represents a complex system of rules and procedures for acting upon and producing sign tokens (Bateson 1972; Kallinikos 1999; Simon 1969). The substantially different orientation of the two technological paradigms raises the question as to whether the principles of functional simplification and closure can really accommodate the computational orientation of information technology and the distinctive character of software as an arrangement of computational rules and procedures.

Despite notable differences, computer-based systems recount, at least to a certain degree, the overall controlling philosophy of technology expressed by the principles of functional simplification and closure. They too involve the selection of an operational domain constructed by the functionalities particular systems embody, and an elaborate system of automated rules and procedures on the basis of which sign tokens and computational relations are established and manipulated. The functionality of particular programs is accomplished through the painstaking elaboration of the computational steps involved, and the closed loops by which such steps are combined into fixed sequences. The vivid debate in the past as regards the simplified character of expert systems and what computers can and cannot do (Dreyfus 2001; Dreyfus and Dreyfus 1986)[6] attests to the fact that

6. Albeit in a different terminology associated with different problems, this debate still goes on and it seems destined to continue for quite a while. See for example Dreyfus (2001) and Hayles (2005).

functional simplification is essential to computer-based technology as well. Given the computational nature of computer-based technologies, it would perhaps seem appropriate to suggest that causal simplification and closure are expressed in the case of these technologies by the related strategies of procedural standardization and cognitive and computational closure.

Procedural standardization is essential to software technology. The user interface and the specific applications mediated by it, which many non-specialists tend to equate with the computer, often encode only a tiny fraction of the highly selective presuppositions embodied in that technology. Technological selectivity is the outcome of an extended series of automated computations sustaining the proper functioning of digital machines that largely obey the logic of cognitive black boxes, descending from the level of the interface to the application and through the operating system down to the very hardware.[7] Clearly, at the level of the application mediated by the user interface, there may exist some discretion as to what steps and procedures (most of which are, of course, pre-programmed) to follow or to choose to enact but not how they will be executed. Below that level, technological processes of token manipulation are completely automated, black-boxed and fenced off from that little zone of discretion at the ordinary user's disposal (Kallinikos 2002; Kittler 1997).

We could thus make a case for the fact that the functional simplification in software-based technology entails the careful demarcation of an operational domain – the functionality of the system or application – and the definition of the operations that embody that functionality. However, functional simplification is predominantly expressed in the layout of the procedural steps and the computations (simplified and closed sequences) that the program embodies. The program itself may be quite complex but the tasks it performs have been substantially cleared of ambiguities and their execution standardized in an elaborate system of largely automated procedures. The brilliant analysis of the limitations of the Von Neumannian games performed by Bateson (1972) is instructive for understanding the nature of the functional simplification and closure underlying particular programs. The problem with Von Neumann's player, Bateson (1972: 285–287) noted, is that it cannot learn from experience.

---

7. See Kittler's associated paper with the evocative title 'There is No Software' (Kittler 1997: 146–155).

Negative outcomes that are due to the player's misperception of the confronted relationships cannot be fed back into the player's cognitive organization. The learning circle is broken. The mathematical fiction that is the player will perform exactly the same way (dictated by the abstract and general character of mathematical relations which the model of the player epitomizes) in the next encounter. Unforeseen relations cannot be handled *in situ*. They could possibly be incorporated into the model by the programmer in a future periodic revision of the program but the player itself cannot respond contingently. The player's response to anticipated event sequences owes much to the computational power of digital machines that allows the pre-programming of a wide variety of scenarios. However, this apparent flexibility or functional ability masks the rigidity of the computational rules and procedures built into the program. Functional simplification is therefore manifested in the closed loops the program performs, the implicit conduit metaphor upon which software engineering is by necessity predicated (Kittler 1997; Lackoff 1995). The learning algorithms currently constructed by the technology of neural networks do not radically alter this situation, even though the claim is often made that they do so. They just push it one step back on the procedural standardization of the learning mechanism, which is but an algorithm (Kallinikos 1998a).[8]

The algorithmic status of programs thus suggests that the technological goals of recurrence and predictability of computer-based systems or artefacts are accomplished through the selection and standardization of the computational operations the program entails, and their procedural execution. Automation of procedures and rules ensure the procedural standardization and cognitive and computational closure of the program. They

---

8. This claim raises some intricate and central questions in artificial intelligence that ultimately call for the explication of what we mean by humans and human learning. Following the development of connectionism, claims have lately been made for constructing software that exhibits epistemic autonomy and emancipation from its programmer, being capable of learning and embodying behaviour whose emergence is not the outcome of a learning algorithm but of the haphazard and unpredictable computations that reflect the software's 'experience' of its encounters with problems. Technologies of this sort are still predominantly at the experimental level. For obvious reasons I cannot deal with these issues here. For an insightful and recent summary see Hayles (2005).

correspond, by and large, to the Luhmannian concepts of functional simplification and closure. Functional closure is furthermore accomplished through the specification of the data requirements (the program admits only certain inputs), cryptography, protocols and other security mechanisms that function as a protective cocoon.

Therefore, for all its difference from industrial technology, the principles of cognitive and computational closure and procedure standardization underlying computer programs restate the basic strategy by which technology as a distinctive regulative regime attempts to deal with the contingent character of the world (Bloomfield and Vurdubakis 2001). Computer programs embody clear rules of reality representation and automated procedures of information processing and inference making (Zuboff 1988). In so doing, they participate in the reproduction of an order in parallel ways to those which Luhmann (1993) subsumes under the labels of functional simplification and closure. That is, they guarantee the recurrence of the operations internal to the system, while their interface with people or with other technologies takes place along closely specified paths – strict input requirements, formation of skill and role profiles and security arrangements – that ensure the reproduction of the program's operations through the exclusion of unwanted interference. It comes then as no surprise that, despite one or another futurological scenario, no major revolutionary claims of a socio-political nature had been tied to computer-based technologies until the rapid diffusion of the internet and the interconnectedness it implies. Little wonder that the growing organizational involvement of computer-based systems has been claimed to have important implications for the design, management and control of organizational operations (see for example Forester 1989; Kling 1996; Orlikowski *et al.* 1996; Zuboff 1988). Yet the claims about major and revolutionary changes in organizational forms and the wider economic and institutional relations sustaining them had to await, by and large, the coming of the internet and the construction of extended zones of interoperability exemplified by large organizational or sector-based information infrastructures.[9]

9. A comparison of Bell's (1976) and Castells's (1996, 2001) works provides evidence of the far greater importance attributed by the latter to information and communications technologies.

2.5 Beyond Boundedness

An understanding of technology in terms of functional simplification and closure is evident, even though the organizational and institutional implications of such an understanding may seem more controversial. As Luhmann (1993) himself suggests, such a view of technology is quite unlikely to be questioned in its basics. What, however, emerges as a key question is: what are the practices and forms by means of which the clear-cut boundaries separating a technological system from its environment are sustained? The crucial character of boundary management emerges clearly against the background of the dynamic character of the contemporary world that is beset with contingencies of every sort, making the construction of predictable and quasi-closed technological systems always a precarious accomplishment. The vital issue increasingly becomes: how can we understand the means by which technology interacts with the 'other side of the form: the immense complexity of causal processes taking their simultaneous course . . . the outside of the form, the foil against which technology is delineated' (Luhmann 1993: 88)?

Placed against the background of the immense complexity of the conditions surrounding technological systems, the project of constructing fully predictable worlds by relying on the controlling strategies of functional simplification and closure could be seen as a rather unattainable ideal. While having far-reaching practical and normative implications, such an ideal always falls short of being fully realized. Frequent technological failures and malfunctioning (Perrow 1984) provide evidence of the limitations of such a project. Control of the internal loops that make up the system is never complete, while the risk of external interference can be reduced but never eliminated. Most crucially, the blind character of the strict couplings technological sequences embody make those contingent events which manage to intrude into the closed circuits of technological interactions, difficult to cope with. Indeed, contingent forces or events that intrude into the technical system may wreak havoc, to the degree that they ride on the intensified and magnified nature of the inscribed causal sequences. Technologically induced accidents give an indication of the magnified forces that, under adverse conditions, manage to escape technological control. Functional simplification and closure reduce the number of causal loops involved but magnify the causal force of the remaining loops. This is an inevitable outcome of the goal of improving the efficiency of the operations which technology helps constitute and regulate. It is therefore inevitable that once the closed and predictable circuit of technological processes is broken, the forces that are set free often have grave or even devastating effects. Nuclear or chemical accidents stand as the epitome here but the pattern can be exemplified by less dramatic accidents like those involved in rail or motorway traffic or the breakdown of industrial devices and systems.

The problem of managing the interface of technology with its environment is a complex issue that has mainly been analysed in terms of control, risk and manageability (Hanseth *et al.* 2001; Kallinikos 2005; Luhmann 1993, 1998). Given technology's inability to repair itself, the crucial question evolves around how to deal technologically with events that manage to intrude into the bounded and protected circuit of technology (Introna 1997). A major response has so far been the construction of ancillary mechanisms of control that have sought to keep human involvement at a minimum. This way, primary technologies have been controlled by second-order technologies which have in turn been monitored by third-order devices and so on. The problem with technological hierarchies of this sort is the transposition of risks at more comprehensive levels, thus tending to produce a new architecture of complexity and risk that trades high frequency/low impact for low frequency/high impact risks (Kallinikos 2005; Luhmann 1993).

The computational constitution of computer-based technology reinforces these traditional strategies of technological control by being crucially involved in the construction of technological hierarchies. Secondary and higher technological control mechanisms are typically provided by computer-based technologies. Nevertheless, the computational constitution of these technologies furnishes a set of conditions that depart significantly from the instrumental enclaves associated with functional simplification and closure. The variety of physical artefacts that traditional technology constructs – or the material sequences embodied in different technological systems – represent discrete, disconnected objects or processes that cannot, as a rule, affect each other. Computation is different in this respect: data produced and managed by different software systems can, in principle, be rendered compatible and interact with each other. Current developments in software technology that facilitate the mixing up, 'mashing-up', of such different artefacts as music, images, maps and texts provide evidence of the possibilities which the computational constitution of technology offers for transcending the specificity of particular technical media, systems or artefacts.

The potential of computation for transcending the functional limits of particular systems or the discrete character of technological artefacts is contingent on the common code language which the irreducible system of just two signs (Borgmann 1999) offers. Differences in constitution or functionalities can be transcended by reconstructing them as combinations (in huge numbers) of binary alternations. The possibility of reducing qualitative differences to a common code language has far-reaching, though evasive, implications operating at the microscopic level of computing (beyond easy observation or user awareness). As I endeavour to show in some detail over the next few pages, such a common code language supports the interpenetration of the functionalities of different software systems in ways unimaginable to traditional technologically-designed, materially-based processes. The interconnected or, perhaps more correctly, interoperable character of computer-based systems and the exchangeability of information produced by means of the huge variety of such systems and applications provides strong evidence that the computational constitution of computer-based technology inaugurates a major technological reorientation. This is a strong claim that needs to be elaborated.

The significance of the interconnected, interoperable character of computer-based systems emerges more forcefully against the background of the technical gaps or discontinuities underlying traditional technological devices or systems. Traditional technologies exhibit an amazing variety of disconnected or incompatible systems and artefacts built on different configurations of principles, means and goals. To some degree this is the outcome of the long, fragmented and locally-contained history of industrialism. But it also reflects the battle of technological imagination to deal with the refractory and heterogeneous character of the physical world, an entirely different project from that of discovering the principles of cognition and embodying them into technical systems and artefacts. It comes then as no surprise that industrialism has been no more than a fragmented landscape of technical islands, the majority of which remain operationally incompatible with one another. Traditional technologies remain functionally incompatible even when they deal with similar tasks, as in the case of rail, air and road traffic systems. Under such conditions functional complementarity (rather than interoperability) is accomplished by letting one system take over at the operational edges of the other. Traditional technologies seldom intersect or merge operationally, as they have been constructed by recourse to different principles, material means and preoccupations. In some cases, like underground and surface rail traffic, such an operational integration may be an issue of appropriate standards. Very often, however, the self-contained nature of different technological systems reflects widely different social and techno-scientific projects, which cannot be reduced to a common code language (the binary system) or an elementary set of principles on the basis of which to transcend the discontinuous and hetero-geneous character of the world.[10]

Now, computer-based systems and technologies may also remain uncoupled or brought to bear upon one another through gateways and other mediating technologies that translate data inputs back and forth from one system to another, yet leave the systems in a tangential relationship with no genuine operational interception. Furthermore, technological path dependencies may lead to lock-ins of technologies that further accentuate the need for backward or sideways compatible innovations. Ultimately, processes of this sort are prone to create independent, self-reinforcing technological trajectories that enhance functionality-based fragmentation of computer-based technologies. Under similar conditions, backward or sideways compatibility becomes a major interoperational issue in large-scale and heterogeneous ensembles of computer-based systems and applications (Bowker and Star 1999; Hanseth 2000, 2004). To these technically driven divisions one must add a variety of social (such as digital exclusions) and institutional (like authentication policies) segmentations which are imposed upon or develop alongside public information infrastructures and the internet, making it a highly fragmented terrain (Introna and Nissenbaum

10.   There is of course a large social and institutional diversity that is impli-
       cated in the operational incompatibility of traditional technologies
       (Hughes 2004). The issue is not strictly technical, yet technical dimensions
       are crucial factors in accounting for the incompatibility of the operations
       of traditional technical artefacts or systems.

1999; Sassen 2004; Woolgar 2002).[11] The incompatibilities, divisions and segmentations that underlie both the internet and other large information infrastructures suggest that it is perhaps naïve to think of them as unified socio-technical platforms along which information, events and benevolent and malevolent acts can smoothly propagate (Bowker and Star 1999; Star and Ruhleder 1994).

The fragmentary landscape of contemporary information and communication technologies and the internet is *prima facie* hard to question. At the same time, it would be useful to distinguish what, for a lack of a better term, I call functional unification, from the interoperability of computer-based technologies. It is beyond any doubt that despite various institutional, social and, to a certain degree, technical barriers, large information infrastructures and the internet contain extended zones of interoperability that, in addition, expand and qualitatively improve over time. This is far from being accidental. Connectivity and interoperability of technological information and the computer-based systems by which information is produced are ultimately rendered possible by the common and continuous cognitive space which the computational nature of computer technology provides (Dreyfus 2001; Kittler 1996, 1997). Some of these trends can be understood along lines suggested by network economics. That is, once a technological innovation reaches (for various reasons) a critical mass of users, it creates its own self-reinforcing patterns of diffusion on the basis of steadily rising returns (Arthur 1988, 1994; Hanseth 2000). In this respect, the significance of the internet, or large organizational and inter-organizational infrastructures, is in establishing its own diffusion momentum, driving internet or infrastructure-compatible organizational information policies that further enhance the interlocking and interoperability of computer-based systems and artefacts worldwide.[12] Insightful as they may be, explanations based on network economics bypass the issue concerning the distinctive computational constitution of computer-based technologies and the extended zones of interoperability that can be constructed on the basis of that constitution. Let me add another slightly modified argument in support of this claim.

11. The difference between surface and deep web is indicative in this respect. See the Appendix at the end of this volume.
12. Some of these issues are treated in some detail in the next chapter.

The computational constitution of computer-based technology and the distinctiveness of software code contrast sharply with the field-based or technically-specific fragmentation of industrial technologies briefly outlined above. The binary character of software code makes all software in principle, if not in practice, mutually compatible. There are no inherent limitations in this respect. Computer-based systems and technologies can potentially be made interoperable, even if they are not so currently. No matter how cumbersome it may be, functional compatibility is always a possibility in software code, a condition that stems from the continuous cognitive space that the computational constitution of that technology described above provides (Borgmann 1999). By contrast, there is no way to merge together the core operations, say, of rail and air traffic technologies, oil refineries and production of electric appliances, or such traditional products or artefacts as films, records or paintings unless they are digitized.[13] Once transformed into the binary code – software – a product or technology can potentially traverse the narrow confines within which it is operating and become an object of communication and exchange within a vast variety of technical and social settings; even though such communication, exchange or manipulation may require additional technical developments or modifications. Music and film piracy and the cracking of software codes by hackers provide evidence of the standing interoperable possibilities of computer-based systems and technologies and the multimedia world of cross-technical zones into which different technologies merge or remediate one another (Bolter and Grusin 2000).[14]

13.   A crucial historical moment towards a common code language prior to Leibniz's discovery of the binary system was Descartes's coordinate system by which he was able to bring together geometric and algebraic representation. Descartes's discovery is very instructive for understanding the logic by which the incommensurable constitution of the real world is transcended. Through his system, different aspects of reality like extension, shape or volume which, since the ancient Greeks, had been considered as distinct and irreducible realms, were brought to bear upon one another. The discontinuous and qualitative differences of aspects of reality could thus be surpassed at the level of mathematical notation by being reduced to the common code language discovered by Descartes (Borgmann 1999: 69–72). See also Goodman (1976, 1978).

14.   The development of so-called mashups provides a good illustration of the potentialities for combining digitally coded data from different sources to create 'one's own' artefacts, for example, mixing up different songs or

The implications of these developments for the traditional strategies of technological control accomplished through functional simplification and closure are far-reaching. Connectivity and interoperability challenge the controlling strategies of functional simplification and closure to the degree that they make the intersection of functionalities and the exchange of data and information across computer-based systems an essential principle of the new technologies (Borgmann 1999). Technological connectivity and interoperability can thus support new forms of transactional interaction. These may involve exchanging and acting upon information, and informatized services and operations across technological and also organizational and institutional boundaries. In so doing they challenge the traditional strategies of technological control and, crucially, the governability of complex socio-technical systems that have been predicated on these strategies. But they also reintroduce contingencies of various kinds into the regulated circuits of technology and make necessary new forms of regulation of the interface of a technological system with its environment (Kallinikos 2005). The rising significance which security arrangements have been acquiring over more than a decade now is indicative in this respect.

2.6 Concluding Remarks

In this chapter, I have suggested that the construction of industrial technological systems has been based upon the logic of functional simplification while their operation has been safeguarded by substantially fencing off this simplified functional order from the surrounding social and environmental complexity. In this respect, industrial technology has furnished a key principle for the management of complex socio-technical assemblages. On the basis of this principle, social and technological operations in organizations have been kept significantly separate from one another and their interaction regulated along highly selective activity corridors. Despite the range of limitations that such a

photographs. See Schofield (2006). Mashups make Marcel Duchamp's almost century-old gesture of exhibiting ready-mades, a gesture aimed at alluding to the end of art in the industrial age, indeed look pale compared to the combinatorial alchemy of 'data ready-mades' which digital technology enables. In the world which digital technology establishes creativity is revealed as just the *ars combinatoria* of fragments that assume the form of digital data feeds.

project is subject to, the instrumental enclosures which this paradigm of industrial technology has built have provided an important part of the infrastructure upon which organizations as bounded and hierarchically unified systems have been predicated (Luhmann 1993; Thompson 1967).

The regulative principles of industrial technology are to some degree reinforced by the computational paradigm. As technologies, computer-based systems and applications cannot but be based on functional simplification and closure. However, computation introduces new principles that ultimately subvert separation and insulation as major strategies of technological regulation. The growing interlocking of a large array of computer-based technologies and the extended zones of interoperability which computation is able to construct violate the premises of functional simplification and closure. I have been at pains to show that technological systems constructed by means of computation may intersect functionally in ways that have not been possible in the case of industrial regimes and technologies. Computation can ultimately reduce the intrinsic heterogeneity of various aspects of the social and natural world (objects, processes, services) to a common denominator which binary coding provides. Software systems, I claim, can always be rendered compatible, no matter how cumbersome the accomplishment of such an objective might be. Thus viewed, computation steps behind the appearance or specific constitution of aspects of reality by cognitively decomposing and reducing them to binary differences. Underneath the distinctive character of things (material and social), a unified principle is discovered (or assumed to exist) by means of which the variability of the world can be recaptured as computationally produced and manipulated information.

The computational constitution of computer-based technology is thus involved in the construction of a pliable reality as the outcome of the rendition of labour and administrative processes as permutable information. Reduced to information, different tasks, procedures or services can be brought to bear upon one another in ways that have not been possible without the functional intersection of different systems which the paradigm of computation enables. The extensive rendition of a large array of tasks and operations as information has contributed to their dissolvability and transferability and further enhanced the intrinsic modern and industrial trends of the disembeddedness of administrative and labour processes. By recasting production and organizational relations in the medium of technological information, the new technologies of information and communication have helped establish some of the preconditions for the decline or, in any case, reframing of boundedness as a major principle of control and the emergence of alternative place- and boundary-transcending forms of organization (Deleuze 1995; Kallinikos 2005).

The fuller appreciation of the organizational and institutional implications of current technological trends makes it necessary to address two complex and demanding analytical problems. The first concerns the analysis and understanding of the almost explosive expansion of information and the consequently increasing significance which information processes have acquired in the course of just a few decades. The organizational implications of the rendition of reality at the level of information and the exchangeability of information across technical and institutional systems are intimately tied to the contemporary growth dynamics of information and the organizational implications such a growth is bound to have. The second requires a thorough treatment of the aforementioned issues concerning the organizational and institutional framework within which current organizational and institutional developments take place. I address these issues in the third and fifth chapters respectively.

3. Information Growth as a Self-Referential Process[1]

Ad Memoria Claudio Ciborra[2]

3.1 Patterns of Information Growth

The spectacular growth of information that has taken place over the last few decades constitutes a major contemporary development that merits close consideration. The profusion of information and its transformation into a key instrument for shaping organizational operations and controlling economic outcomes have had important implications that will become even more profound in the future. Such a belief is reinforced by the current patterns of information growth that seem to be acquiring escalating qualities (Lyman *et al.* 2003). Beyond the hype that has often obscured an unpressured appreciation of these developments, the acute observer cannot fail to see that, in its current phase, information and the technologies and structures by which it is supported are no longer, if they ever were, the subservient means to any ends. Rather, they form a complex constellation of

---

1. A substantially shorter version of this chapter has been published in *Information Technology and People*, see Kallinikos 2006a. The present text has been reworked and expanded in a number of significant ways. It is not only a more elaborate but in many respects a quite different text.
2. Claudio Ciborra died prematurely on 13 February 2005 at the age of 53. He was the head of the Department of Information Systems at the London School of Economics and Political Science and a major intellectual figure in the cross-disciplinary field of information systems, economics and organization studies. In the spring of 2002 he asked me to review the interdisciplinary literature on risk and information technology and produce a text that could serve as a means for constructing a conceptual framework to deploy in a major project on risk and technology that he was heading together with Ole Hanseth at the University of Oslo. When I started that journey I had no idea where it would take me. As I discovered, it opened a new intellectual agenda for me. Many of the ideas presented in this text originated in that literature review and it feels right to dedicate this chapter to Claudio's memory.

practices, orientations and techniques that increasingly impose their own recalcitrant actuality. I have already outlined some of the implications that ensue from the rendition and reconstitution of reality as information. Due to the complicated character of the issues involved however, I have deliberately refrained from introducing a straightforward confrontation with the dynamics of information growth, so characteristic of the contemporary world. Nevertheless, there is no way of obtaining an adequate picture of current developments without addressing these issues. The technological, organizational and institutional implications that were considered in the two preceding chapters may well be only a fraction of a much more profound and long-wave change of which information growth forms an integral part.

Looked at on a larger timescale, the cornucopia of information emerges as a distinctive mark of the late twentieth/early twenty-first centuries (Brown and Duguid 2000; Hylland-Eriksen 2001). The expansive ferment of information suggests that its fast pace of growth is unlikely to abate in the years to come. On the contrary, it would be reasonable to expect the patterns of information growth to gather speed and diversify (Hylland-Eriksen 2001; Lyman *et al.* 2003; Shiller 2003) as new activities or domains of social life, rendered as technological information, enter the circuits of digitized computation and communication at an accelerating pace.[3] Because every activity or domain of contemporary life that becomes informatized does not expand the amount of information solely in proportion to the new data its informatization brings to the digitized circuits. The relationship between the old and new data is seldom additive. Over the extended zones of interoperability which contemporary technology constructs, data from a large variety of sources can be combined in an equally large variety of ways with other data,

3.   In their report Lyman *et al.* (2003) estimate that between 1999 and 2002 new stored information more than doubled, growing at about 30 per cent per year. The same authors count the production of new information in 2002 as five exabytes. These numbers are of such a magnitude that they elude the human sense of quantity. I quote them: 'If digitized, the nineteen million books and other print collections in the (US) Library of Congress would contain about ten terabytes of information; five exabytes of information is equivalent in size to the information contained in half a million new libraries the size of the Library of Congress print collections', see http://www.sims.berkeley.edu/research/projects/how-much-info-2003/index.htm. See also the Appendix at the end of this volume.

thereby increasing substantially the amount of information that
can be produced. There exist of course a variety of technical,
institutional   and   also   cultural   (behavioural   and
meaning-related) barriers to such a combinatorial alchemy.[4]
Even when these powerful constraints are taken into account, a
large number of combinatorial options still remain open, some of
which are, sooner or later, bound to be attempted (Ciborra 2006;
Shiller 2003).

These introductory remarks suggest that the issues associated
with the expansion and fast growth of information are many,
complex and intriguing. It is vital to approach and understand
these phenomena in ways that do justice to their complexity and
far-reaching implications. Rather than being the outcome of
haphazard incidents, the expansion and growth of information
is a systemic and for that reason intrinsic characteristic of the
contemporary world. It is closely associated with sophisticated
storage and updating mechanisms, the online availability and
the combinability of technological information that coincide
with an increasingly interoperable ecology of computer-based
technologies. There is a complex pattern of mutual implication
of information with the technologies by which it is produced
and mediated, whereby the one reinforces the other, in an iterative cycle of interactive sequences. The expansion and growth of
information are mediated by an increasing array of sophisticated
information processing and communication technologies. In
turn, such an expansion and growth of information feeds back
on technological development by acting as the springboard for
further diffusion and the social or organizational embeddedness
of these technologies as a means of organizing, taking advantage
of and generally dealing with data and information.

The ideas presented in this chapter draw from a variety of
social science disciplines to develop an explanatory account of
the relevant developments that construes information processes
as basically self-propelling and, in some respects, escalating.
Despite the mounting significance of these developments, we
seem to lack adequate theoretical explanations of this complex
and, in a sense, 'out-of-control' character of information growth

---

4. Cultural barriers arise out of the meaningfulness of data combinations. It
   does not perhaps make sense to combine data about agricultural production with crime, as combinations of this sort are culturally irrelevant. Such
   cultural relevancies are however shifting over time.

processes. Information expansion and growth are increasingly taking place in larger ecosystems composed of practices, tasks, information structures and technologies interacting in ways that usually extend beyond the immediate inspection and control of particular agents and organizations, and their local pursuits. The complexity and interdependent character of these processes suggests that only a limited portion of these developments can be attributed to deliberate actions and the intentions or goals of social agents. Even less comprehensive processes like the design, development or implementation of information systems in particular settings can only be partly understood as a process of local accommodation or adaptation (Hanseth and Braa 2000; March 1994; March and Olsen 1989). For these reasons, it is necessary to study the dynamics of information growth in ways that step beyond simple instrumentalist or agency-centric accounts of information as interpretation and be able to accommodate wider processes taking place across local contexts and not infrequently behind the backs of social agents (Esposito 1996, 2003; Searle 1995).

After a brief depiction of the relevant definitions and conceptual clarifications, the overwhelming bulk of this chapter is dedicated to the exposition of three major claims advanced to account for the expanding and partly escalating growth patterns of information. First, the dynamics of information expansion and growth are construed as being closely associated with the self-referential, non-foundational constitution of information. This is an elusive and in a sense counter-intuitive claim, whose exposition involves a series of complex and abstract theoretical arguments. In particular, the conception of information in self-referential and non-foundational terms contrasts sharply with the widely diffused view that portrays information as just the last or epiphenomenal step in the description or representation of a reference domain (see for example, Devlin 2001). Regardless of whether such an account is predicated on a realist or nominalist understanding of social processes of perception or cognition, it fails to disclose the interrelated, structurally conditioned character of the relevant processes, and the decisive fact that contemporary information growth dynamics involves to a considerable degree the generation of information out of information (Zuboff 1988). Second, the expansion and growth of information is posited as being crucially related to the diffusion and involvement of computer-based technologies. This self-referential character of information growth can, to a substantial degree, be attributed to the availability of technological data and its combinability or permutability across systems, databases and organizations. Third, contemporary information growth dynamics reflect an institutionally orchestrated game for obtaining information that is fresh and relevant. However, such a game inevitably results in information becoming readily depreciated and obsolete, thereby setting up a complex institutional process for maintaining and expanding the informativeness of information. Manifested in various ways for storing, processing, updating and recombining information, the objective of maintaining the informativeness of information is essentially contributing to the self-propelling, runaway character (Arthur 1988) of information expansion and growth.

3.2   Definitions and Conceptual Clarifications

In its current use, information is predominantly understood as a doubly-constituted entity, entailing the cognitive and material operations by means of which sign tokens are generated and organized to carry semantic content, that is, meaning. Information as semantic content can neither be generated nor be conveyed to others without recourse to the materiality of sign tokens, for example, oral, written, or material, analogue or digital. Cultural signs are however themselves the product of social practices, as the case of alphabetic or numeric tokens demonstrates (Searle 1995).[5] Indispensable as they are, signs must be placed within the social practice or tradition to which they belong to yield their signifying function. Information generation is therefore a semantic process that cannot be reduced to the sign tokens by which it is generated. The diffusion of technological information has, however, blurred what may have seemed a clear distinction in the first place. By separating information processes from interaction and communication,[6] and embodying them in technologically controlled rules and procedures (that is, the software), computer-based technology has, in many respects, rendered the difference between information and its material

---

5. A distinction can be made between natural signs (for example, thunder indicating rain) and cultural signs (for example, alphabetic marks, figures, images). I predominantly deal with cultural signs in this text. For an overview see Borgmann (1999), Eco (1976) and Leach (1976).
6. See the preceding chapter.

substratum less pronounced.[7] Can data produced out of other data through automated rules and procedures be considered to be information? The answer is not straightforward and a significant part of this chapter is dedicated to the examination of these issues.

If information is a semantic phenomenon, how does it differ from all other cognitive or cultural activities (that is, art and knowledge) that are also involved in the creation and maintenance of meaning? Accounting for differences between these fundamental domains of social and cultural life may well necessitate a series of separate treatises, as the work of Kant and his followers demonstrates (Casirrer 1955). But even though such a project cannot be pursued here, it is necessary to advance a few key distinctions as a means of disentangling information from knowledge or those aspects of art that have been seen as being closely associated with cognition (see for example Arnheim 1971; Goodman 1976, 1978, 1984). I propose two key elements that confer on information its special status and distinguish it from knowledge and cognition; its a) temporally-bound and b) contingent or event-like character. Both combine to make information heavily dependent on the quality of 'news' it is capable of carrying. Let me explain.

Information differs substantially with respect to the degree to which it informs. Obviously, all information does not have the same value. Differences in value are closely tied to the temporally limited character of information and the degree to which it can unearth or disclose the event-like character of minute life episodes. In order to be informative, information must be able to add a distinction and confer something new on what is already known. In this respect, the value of information, what may be

7. Another way of framing the issue is to say that semantic information differs from the signal organization and the rule-based manipulations of syntactic tokens which in technological information are the domain of the engineering of information. Even if one accepts the common claim, already advanced by information theory's founding fathers (Shannon and Weaver 1949), that semantics is irrelevant to engineering aspects of information (that is, data) while the latter may always impact on the former, it is nonetheless legitimate, indeed imperative, to study the dynamics of information growth at both levels. The understanding of information in terms of semantics should not, however, be confused with the agency-centric interpretation of data tokens. I take up these issues throughout this text and I dedicate the next chapter exclusively to discussing the relationship between meaning, subjectivity and interpretation.

called its informativeness,[8] is indeed a function of the kind of 'news' it is capable of conveying, and 'news' differs substantially with respect to what it adds to that which is already known. As a rule, the value of 'news' is traceable to its unique (contingency) and novel (time) character. Conveying something which is already known is to communicate no information, no matter how important (in ethical, cultural or other terms) such a message may be. As Borgmann (1999: 133) expresses, 'to be told that the sun will rise tomorrow is to receive no information. To learn that one has won the jackpot in the lottery is to have great news.' In this respect, time and contingency are intrinsically tied to information.

The value of information is heavily dependent on what exists on the other side of the equation, that is, the individuals or agents to whom information makes sense and informs. What is useful information to one individual may be completely worthless to another. As truthful as such a view *prima facie* may appear, it is often of restricted value in understanding the role of information in the contemporary world. In collective settings, like those which organizations or markets represent, the informativeness of information is defined against the background of practices and needs of larger groups. What is of value to the individual may be worthless to the organization, for the information needs of organizations may gain little from individual revelations that do not contribute to the stock of collective information. Similarly, the economic value of information emerges against the background of the 'news' it carries to a collectivity and seldom to particular individuals. In this respect, information has an objective (or inter-subjective) life similar to that of money or language. That is, what is useful is useful to anyone despite differences in the subjective perceptions of usefulness. Indeed, in many cases information, like money, is of value to those that already possess information of one kind or another and can distinguish between needs which available information fails to satisfy. The relationship of information to itself is the major subject of this chapter, but before I embark on this theme, the differences between knowledge and information require clarification.

Knowledge has often been treated in the literature as akin, if

8.   Defined by the *Oxford English Dictionary* as 'The quality or condition of being informative'.

not as synonymous, to information. To a certain extent this is reasonable, in so far as both knowledge and information are distinctive cognitive phenomena entailing coextensive regions in which the one implicates the other, that is, information may add to the stock of knowledge while the usefulness of the former often depends on the latter. On the other hand, knowledge differs from information in the sense that it resists the inescapable depreciation that time normally confers upon information. As a rule, knowledge entails elaborate and durable cognitive structures that form the basis upon which the world is comprehended (for example, the sun will rise tomorrow). The durable character of these structures suggests that knowledge cannot adequately be understood in terms of novelty and the quality of 'news' Borgmann's aforementioned statement rightly attributes to information, even though the difference could be seen as one of degree rather than of kind. After all, little can survive the passage of time and the ravages it brings.

In view of a widespread conflation of information with knowledge prevailing in the literature, it is crucial to reiterate that information is not a measure of the cultural, moral or even cognitive importance of a message but rather an indicator of the newness it carries. Information may differ from knowledge in several respects, yet a major difference pivots around the short-lived and contingent status of information as distinct from the value of knowledge closely associated with the discovery of regularities or patterns that persist over larger timescales. Knowledge, being tacit or formal, may change as the result of either the reorganization of experience (that is, tacit knowledge) or the reformulation of the theories by which it is supported (that is, formal knowledge). Neither of these changes occurs as the result of knowledge losing its newness, for knowledge is not defined, at least not predominantly, by its newness. By contrast, information is depreciated to the degree that it is divested from its basic quality of being informative and the difference such a quality makes, as the result of the 'news' it carries (Borgmann 1999).

The 'news' information carries does not necessarily imply that those states or relationships it refers to, that is, the content of information, are about the present or take place in the present. What does take place in the present is the generation of information itself, for the meaning of information emerges against the background of social concerns and relevancies as these are perceived in the present. Old information, or more correctly stored data, may be upgraded to information by being retrieved or reprocessed in ways that make sense to social agents in the present. Data may therefore re-emerge as information by being reinserted and made to bear upon the web of relevancies that constitute the present. In this respect, the production of information is bound up with the present, and the quality of 'news' it carries is inescapably related to the contemporaneous pursuits of social agents. What information stands for may, however, concern states or relationships of the past (a very distant past indeed) or even an imagined future. The significance information assumes in the contemporary world is variously related to the strong orientation of this age towards the present (as opposed to the past and future), which does imply a priority for information content capturing contemporaneous events or states. However, there is no intrinsic relationship between time horizon and information content.[9]

These observations bring us to another controversial and, I think, often misunderstood issue between scholars who reject the engineering view of information as simply the manipulation of syntactic tokens. I discuss these issues in some detail in the next chapter but some clarifications are necessary at this point. It should be obvious that information as a semantic phenomenon is tied to social agents and a distinction should accordingly be made between data and information. As opposed to data, information emerges out of the living encounters of social agents with data while its meaning is shaped by their concerns, activities and preoccupations. True as this is, it shouldn't imply that information growth processes could exclusively be accounted for in agency-centric terms. On the one hand, technological information makes data available in a large variety of ways, multiplying and thickening the points of contact social agents have with data. In so doing technological information vastly raises the possibility of *ad hoc* information generation processes in which the sheer technological availability of data is both a prerequisite and an important driving force for these processes. On the other hand, information growth at aggregate levels is the outcome of a multitude of initiatives, many of which support, criss-cross or undermine one another. The forms by which these

9. I take up this subject in section 3.5, in which I discuss the short-lived and disposable character of information.

initiatives interact and influence each other exhibit emergent properties that make their aggregate outcome seldom straight-forwardly traceable to the objectives of particular agents and the strong financial or other kinds of interests they may pursue.

The automated character of second-order processing (for example, search engines, data mining and profiling, portals) further blurs the distinction between data and information, making the attribution of aggregate information processes to particular agents a rather heroic assumption. Little wonder that second-order software encodes highly selective presuppositions as regards to the way data is processed, organized and presented. Powerful social agents may accordingly influence substantially the formation of aggregate processes, as the cases of Yahoo and Google and the interests they co-opt exemplify (Introna and Nissenbaum 2000). 'Artefacts have politics' as Winner (1986) has gracefully put it. I take it as given that the participation of social agents is crucial to understanding key elements of the current information growth dynamics. But social agents are not exogenous to these processes even though it often makes sense to treat them as such. They are not outside the current information growth dynamics controlling the relevant processes from a position that theology once reserved for god. Their interests, perceptions, goals and preoccupations are shaped, often defined by a great array of factors among which the current state of technology development is crucial. Google was technologically impossible a little more than a decade ago. As I seek to demonstrate in the next three sections of this chapter, current information growth dynamics exhibit characteristics and growth patterns that, considered over larger time spans, appear to elude even powerful agents.

3.3 Information Processes and Self-Reference

Information could be seen as involving descriptions of facts, relationships or states in a reference domain in ways that are capable of conferring some novelty, no matter how tiny, on what is already known or available. A reference domain may not necessarily be limited to referential reality, that is, to things and humans. It may well extend to descriptions of other descriptions and descriptions of descriptions of other descriptions. As we will soon see this is a critical quality for understanding the processes of information growth. A referential fact is rendered information whenever an operation, activity or state is transposed on to a medium, for example, oral, written or electronic as this may be. When a bank client's transaction at an automatic teller is rendered as information, then a referential fact is recorded providing an account of an act and its context, that is, the identity of the client, the volume, time and place of the transaction and so forth. The same holds true when a medical or criminal incident is added to an existing database of medical or criminal facts. As these examples suggest, information is often the outcome of technologically-sustained routines through which an impressive array of details (events), with only a modest or little degree of newness, are recorded in organized data fields. Deployed this way, information records 'life', allowing actors and organizations to keep track of their operations in a fairly routine and repetitive way.

An interesting relationship emerges at this point. As soon as the fabric of life is transposed into information, it provides the foundation on to which new information can be built, through not necessarily the new rendition of referential facts or states. Rather, information can be generated through the very insertion of recorded facts into the greater picture of available information about similar or relevant facts. Such a picture can itself be composed in several ways. A client's transactions, for instance, can be related to her/his transactions during the last week, month or year, or be compared to the transactions of other bank clients during that day or week and so forth. Similarly, a criminal or medical incident can be related to available criminal or medical information to provide new information about criminal or medical facts, or even brought to bear upon other available information to produce profiles such as the geographic or demographic distribution of criminal or medical facts. A large variety of such combinations is usually available. Which of these combinations will become actualized depends to some degree on the characteristics of the contexts within which they occur and the interests and preoccupations of local agents. Or they may arise, as often happens, as the outcome of haphazard and contingent processes that cannot be predicted in advance. Furthermore, some of these combinations are currently produced on a routine basis across local contexts through specifically-tailored information systems (for example, profiling and data mining applications), a condition that makes the attribution of these combinations to the meaning-induced choices of locally embedded agents only one out of several information generating processes.

Organized information therefore has a dual value, that is, a) as an informatized rendition (a description) of a particular aspect of a reference domain and b) as a relationship such a description bears or may develop to already available descriptions. Correspondingly, a description of descriptions, that is, a meta-description, may entertain a relationship with other meta-descriptions. It is thus of crucial importance to point out that newly-generated information does not simply add or record a new fact or state. It modifies and reframes, and not infrequently in a decisive way, the value of already existing information, which can thus be interpreted in a new light. These processes are well-exemplified by the current prospects facing financial and insurance services, as the outcome of the opportunity to bring information pieces deriving from different sources to bear upon one another (Shiller 2003). Combining information from different data sources enables, Shiller suggests, the development of tailor-made (as opposed to standardized) financial and insurance services thanks to the ability to correlate data items across continuously updated databases,[10] for example, income tax returns, data on consumer expenditures, mortgages, travel habits, other demographic or medical data and so forth. New information on individual life patterns, which tailor-made services to some degree presuppose, is emerging not solely on the basis of recording particular facets of an individual's life but crucially through the very comparison, juxtaposition and combination of data across information sources and databases. Simple or straightforward as it may be, this systemic or, perhaps more correctly, structural view of information provides a fruitful path for understanding the self-referential and increasingly expanding forms through which contemporary processes of information develop.[11]

Collectively, these observations suggest that every time a new information item (or series of items) is brought to bear upon an already existing information corpus, it creates the possibility of

10. Global and continuously updateable databases that are deployed as a means of providing background knowledge for the making of insurance policies on the basis of risk analysis are sometimes referred to as GRID (Global Risk Information Databases) technologies (Shiller 2003: ch. 14).
11. This argument bears, it should be noted, a strong affinity with structuralism in linguistics and semiotics (see for example, Eco 1976; Leach 1976).

establishing a novel cognitive pattern or relationship which was not there at the beginning. Given that an information item could enter into a relationship with more than just one item in a dataset, it is understandable that even a moderate addition of information items to even a modest information system could lead to the exponential growth of the information contained in that system, even in the presence of strong combinability constraints. As already indicated in the introduction to this chapter, constraints of this sort usually arise for technological, organizational/institutional or behavioural reasons (Brown and Duguid 2000; March 1994) but they are themselves subject to change and modification.

The structural constitution of information and the self-referential information growth it induces provide a set of conditions that can contribute to explaining why information processes are intrinsically tied to unintended consequences that may betray the purpose of certainty and control that instigated them in the very first place. Information generated to illuminate and also control specific aspects of reality may result, through its recombination with existing information sources, in the creation of a new picture that may come to challenge established truths quite radically. Information growth does not have these dramatic effects every day, but incremental changes do bring qualitative changes from time to time, some of which may in fact have far-reaching and unintended consequences. While information generated for particular purposes may lead to increasing control of those aspects of reality by which it has been motivated, it may also increase rather than reduce uncertainty with respect to wider processes, an outcome that is often difficult to anticipate in advance (Beck 1992; Beck *et al.* 1996; Luhmann 1993). In this sense, information processes may be said to entail a relatively epistemic autonomy from the interests and preoccupations of social agents, often taking them aback.

As paradoxical and counter-intuitive as the relationship of information to certainty may sound, it ultimately reflects the non-foundational nature of information that Bateson (1972) defined some time ago as 'a difference that makes a difference'. Differences by necessity emerge through the juxtaposition or comparison of two or more items or objects. Differences, Bateson (1972) suggests, are not singular entities located in discrete objects (material or cognitive) but relationships between objects that emerge as different from one another with respect to one or another property (see also Cooper 2005). The non-foundational nature of information suggests that the relationship between information and certainty (as a description of reality) is not exogenous (Bateson 1972; Cooper 1986; Derrida 1978). Information does not simply arise out of descriptions of the solid world of things that can be derived from information through its exhaustive rendition into organized sign tokens. The amount of information contained in reality is not finite because it is not an attribute of that reality alone, but also of the type and discriminatory power of the sign systems deployed to describe that reality. The more fine grained the distinctions which signs carry, the more reality is discovered within reality, that is, the richer the description of that reality becomes (Kallinikos 1996). There is, in other words, a constitutive relationship between means of representation and the represented domain, between the rendition of the world as information and the world itself. Information thus partakes in the construction of reality, providing descriptions of it that may lead to the counter-intuitive yet frequent outcome whereby information tends to raise rather than diminish uncertainty.

The self-referential and self-propelling character of information processes suggests that the game of information is thus constituted so that the deficit is always on the side, so to speak, of the responses which information itself is supposed to supply. While incoming data may address well-specified information needs, it cannot help, by virtue of being related to other data, but disclose new aspects of reality that raise novel questions, begging further information search and so on (Bateson 1972; Eco 1976; Luhmann 2002). Hardware and software standardization further accentuate these trends by rendering information recombinable across a wide variety of systems and contexts. In the following section I consider ways through which technologically-based information processes are pushing these runaway information processes to their limit. Before we turn to this task, it is important to stress that the self-propelling dynamics of information growth are constitutive of the game of information. The unpredictable consequences of information generation could be seen as side effects, if by this term is meant the unintended consequences accompanying the actions of a particular group of agents or even by society in its entirety. Yet side effects are systemically induced, forming an intrinsic (rather than accidental) outcome of this game.

This last observation forces us to introduce further qualification to the original argument advanced here. For expository reasons, I have suggested above that information has a dual constitution, as a description of a certain fact or state and as the relationship which that description bears to already available descriptions. In fact, what I term *description* is itself a relationship between items, albeit much more elusive and easy to overlook (Bateson 1972). A description is no more than a package of differences, black-boxed by the seemingly autonomous character of the description which its meaning helps establish (Esposito 1996). Such a simple entity as a word is composed of different syllables which can be traced down to differences between letters, and so on. In this respect, information is but a web of binary differences, some of which are organized hierarchically in terms of more or less inclusive information items or structures which are underneath constituted as no more than other webs of differences, until everything is traced down to the binary constitution of computational information.

The capacity of computer-based technology to reduce all differences to the common denominator of binary alternations emerges more clearly when juxtaposing digital and analogue forms of representation. In analogue representation, differences may not be, and usually are not, scalable down to the level of binary or discrete elements and their combinations on the basis of rules or conventions. Analogue pictorial representation, for instance, is not composed of distinct and standardized marks and cannot thus be decomposed into primary elements (Goodman 1976, 1978; Kallinikos 1996, 2002). It is for this reason that computationally-generated (digital) information has the potential of overcoming the intrinsic heterogeneity and incommensurability of artefacts, both tangible and cognitive, that are based on analogue modes of representation. By dissolving reality to its primary substratum, computation (re)discovers the unifying principle (binary differences) by which it can be rendered commensurable as information.[12] This is the reasoning that Kittler (1997) summarized in his evocative and provocative paper *There is No Software*, which carries forward to the modern technological sphere the inheritance of the claims once made

12. Recall the analysis undertaken in the preceding chapter concerning the differences between, on the one hand, traditional, materially-based and, on the other hand, digital technologies.

famous by the structuralist notion of the double articulation of language (see for example Barthes 1967; Kallinikos 1993).[13] Consider the following illuminating passage from Borgmann (1999: 60), in which he takes up this theme in the context of discussing Plato's dialogue *Philebus*:

> To be able to identify marks on papers (as letters), one has to know how each letter, in an alphabet of 26 capital letters, differs from all the other twenty-five letters. Every letter has a twenty-fivefold distinctiveness. An R differs from an A in having a rounded upper part. It differs from B in having a straight line where the B has a lower roundedness. And so for all the remaining letters. Socrates must have had something like this in mind when he concluded his account of how Theuth discovered the digital nature of letters: 'Perceiving, however, that none of us could learn any one of them alone by itself without learning them all and considering that this was a common bond which made them all one, he assigned to them a single science and called it grammar.'

I have dwelled at some length on the exposition of the non-foundational constitution of information as difference that makes a difference because it provides the conceptual underpinnings for understanding the growth of information out of information. It is unlikely that the complexity and ramifications of current information growth dynamics would be understood without serious consideration of the non-foundational constitution of information and the self-referential patterns it is associated with. To the degree, then, that contemporary computational technology overcomes the incompatibilities of older information sources that remained separate for, at least, technical reasons, it also vastly expands the potential of information growth. This leads us to the subject of the next section.

3.4 The Permutability of Technological Information

The pattern of generating information out of information described above is substantially enhanced by the increasing degree of permutability underlying technological information.

---

13. Language is doubly articulated in the sense of being composed of the discrete elements of letters and syllables which comprise a primary level of organization that is devoid of meaning and a second level from words upwards where signification and meaning emerge, weaving as one ascends to the level of the sentence and the discourse their fascinating and complex texture (see Ricoeur 1977).

There are usually a large number of ways that data items can be related to one another within and across databases and sources. The selection of a context on which an information item or chunk can impact is conditioned by a variety of technological or quasi-technological factors (for example, standardization, compatibility of measurement systems, relevance of the reference domains) that impact on data combinability. Constraints of this sort are shifting, however. Over the last two decades, substantial barriers to combinability across data sources and media (voice and image) have been lifted and the relevant developments are continuously gathering momentum as different technologies and media are mixed up.

Information combinability is also conditioned by a variety of social, cultural and institutional factors. The social practices and work patterns within which information processes develop play an important role in this respect (Brown and Duguid 2000; Ciborra and Lanzara 1994; Orlikowski 2000). Routines and the patterns of meaning in which organizational operations are embedded shape the forms by which already available information is acted upon, recycled, explored or recombined. Given the institutional and behaviourally conservative character of routines and standard operating procedures, it is reasonable to expect that the production of information out of information takes place along paths that have become engraved by the repetitive identification of information needs and the use of information (Brown and Duguid 2000; March 1994; March and Olsen 1989). For routines, habits and established structural mechanisms or interaction patterns frame the practical concerns of social agents and ultimately provide the horizon of meaning against which the combinatorial possibilities of information as a means of disclosing novel conditions are explored. In this respect, the nature of established practices, the structural arrangements supporting them and the routines they are associated with function as stabilizing mechanisms by means of which only a portion, perhaps a very limited one, of what is possible within a given information space is explored.

Routines and social practices are not immune to technological change, however. As indicated several times already, the involvement of computer-based technologies in organizational and institutional life expands the production and dissemination of information and, in this respect, influences the perception of reality while enabling control and communication at a distance.

New systems and the information they make available, sooner or later induce new practices and habits either as a means of accommodating the expanding information or as a means of pursuing new goals and opportunities (Postman 1992). The growth of a large array of new electronically supported services across the private and public sector (for example, e-government) over the last two decades represents an instance of this expanding developmental cycle. Most crucially perhaps, information generation in organizations or other settings of the contemporary world occurs within elaborate, socially organized, technologically sustained information systems or infrastructures that exhibit a significant degree of standardization across applications and systems (Bowker and Star 1999; Ciborra 2000). The often patchy character of information infrastructures notwithstanding, it is crucial to recognize that information processes that run on even modestly standardized information infrastructures considerably expand the combinability of information items and reframe the patterns of social perception with respect to what is considered possible, useful or relevant.

Information growth could, to a certain degree, be accounted for by the incremental and locally-induced changes precipitated by the growing involvement of computer-based technologies in terms of information availability and the mechanisms for acting upon information itself (Zuboff 1988). A closer examination of current developments, however, suggests that information infrastructures grow out of the complex interaction of technological and institutional forces operating at an aggregate level. The control of these processes evades the inspecting capacity of situated agents and can only modestly be attributed to deliberate planning or human conservatism. The spectacular growth of the internet and other private or non-public information infrastructures stands as the epitome of these complex and only partly controlled patterns of information growth. Once available, information tends to induce technological innovations within and across organizations, as a means to the more effective ordering and processing of information (Beniger 1986; Brown and Duguid 2000). Technological innovations, in turn, establish favourable conditions for further information growth and access. Sooner or later, the interaction of technology and information obtains a life of its own, whereby what is available or possible gains precedence over the choice of courses of action based on the careful analysis of information needs. Available solutions (technologies) define problems rather than the other way around (March and Olsen 1976, 1989). The diffusion patterns of Enterprise Systems (or ERP systems) over the last decade or so represents a good approximation of this process (see for example Fleck 1994; Kallinikos 2004b). These trends are no doubt strengthened by the significant commercial interests of software developers and vendors and the trends of normative or mimetic isomorphism whereby organizations tend to adopt technological packages, either as a way to respond to dominant norms and cultural schemes in their environment or as a means to catch up with competitors (Powell and DiMaggio 1991).

Technologically generated information reinforces the self-propelling spiral of information in various ways. It does so through the magnified capacity of computer-based systems to record events or states and to process information. Technological processing of information is indeed a form of producing information out of information that is controlled, at least for a limited period of time, by the automation of the rules (that is, predetermined forms of combining information items embodied in the software) for processing information. But as experience suggests (see for example Hanseth and Braa 2000; Ciborra 2006), the proliferation of information demands, sooner or later, new systems with greater capacity and more complex rules for acting upon information. At an aggregate level, the transition from simple and functionally isolated computer-based systems to large-scale interoperable information infrastructures provides a good illustration of the process whereby the proliferation of information and technological innovation reinforce one another in an expanding spiral (Bowker and Star 1999; Ciborra 2000). Furthermore, computer-based technologies are instrumental in constructing an organizational and work environment where information reaches down to the most minute fabric of everyday operations (Kallinikos 2004b; Zuboff 1988), increasingly engulfing the carrying out of small tasks which left little or no information traces before (Rolland and Monteiro 2002). In all these ways, technological information establishes the very conditions that lead to its further growth.

Less obvious perhaps are those developments whereby computer-based technologies manage to overcome some of the limitations of the older forms of information generation and processing that left paper-based classification and information systems, by and large, functionally incompatible or independent. Despite the fact that technologically sustained information infrastructures remain to a certain degree patchy and closed through regulatory practices and corporate or sector-based firewalls (Sassen 2004), they are involved in various ways in the homogenization of the available information sources. They promote standardized principles of information recording and ordering that are often motivated by or at least make possible the crossing of the boundaries of specific and operationally independent information systems or datasets. Hyperlinks become the technological form by which search engines carry this logic to its extreme limit. According to this logic, any information item can be brought to bear upon any other possible item, without the semantic limitations and technical incompatibilities that have as a rule underpinned older information generation and processing practices.

Interoperability, of which hyperlinks are just a surface manifestation, is a major ideal in the contemporary technologically sustained information systems (Ciborra 2006; Shiller 2003) that is crucially related to the runaway dynamics of information growth (Hanseth *et al.* 2001) that I seek to describe in this chapter. Interoperable systems contrast sharply with the functional and institutional segmentation which paper- and traditional computer-based systems of information processing have occasioned. As Dreyfus (2001: 9–12) suggests, older classification and information systems remained heavily tied to particular social practices and the specific kind of activities associated with them, for example, medical or library science and the practices they gave rise to. By necessity, each system grew as the outcome of such practices, which ultimately provided the horizon of meaning within which information was generated and used. Most crucially, such practices defined the social and cultural relevance of information and, by extension, the boundaries which the information thus generated or used could seldom transcend. Boundaries of this sort were further reinforced by the incompatible classification and ordering principles social practices embodied, and the technical simplicity of paper-based and early computerized systems that did not often allow for the crossbreeding of information (Bowker and Star 1999). By breaking the self-stabilizing and functionally independent character of social practices, technologically interoperable information brings to apotheosis the possible permutations of information items, and thus bolsters and ultimately escalates the processes by which information grows. These are, in fact, the quasi-technical (computational) foundations underlying the immense expansion of the internet and large-scale information infrastructures.

These processes are further reinforced by the increasing technological sophistication of a growing number of computer-based systems and applications. The awareness of the relatively open nature of permutations enabled by the standardized character of technological information is manifested in the rapidly growing number of technological applications (meta-devices) for extracting information out of information. Apart from the diffusion of a variety of forms and meta-devices (second and third order devices) like portals and search engines for organizing and processing information, the rapid diffusion of data mining and profiling techniques provides sufficient evidence of the permutability of information and its self-propelling character. New information is, in the case of profiling techniques, produced by identifying those relations between data items that are believed to exist in databases but which remain hidden or buried under the vast amount of data contained therein. Despite the fact that associations between information items are in such cases guided by an overall purpose (often spotting behavioural patterns in recorded transactions such as money laundering or consumer preferences), the methods by which such associations are constructed are similar to those of the search engines, that is, syntactic associations made possible through formal classification systems and algorithmic techniques. The overall outcome of these developments is to increase substantially the number of possible permutations at the same time as it adds new permutable information output to the available information sources.

These observations suggest that technological information can be recombined into new patterns largely by recourse to specifically tailored software, which due to its technical superiority expands significantly the generation of new information. In this respect, the exploration of already available information manually is subject to powerful limitations. The sheer volume of data indicates that the manual exploration of information is bound to be shallow and will not represent a viable strategy other than in individual cases (Hylland-Eriksen 2001). The speed by which data mining and profiling software or search engines can run across huge databases suggests that the permutability of the technologically available information will both be enabled and constrained (patterned) by the rules through which specific software-based techniques manipulate syntactic information tokens. Yet the capacity of these techniques to manipulate data tokens constantly expands as their short history well demonstrates. It may appear cynical, and in a certain respect unfortunate, yet these trends suggest that in the technological world of the information age, form takes precedence over content and procedure over meaning. They do so to a degree that makes the ordering and often-criticized strategies of modernity and its institutions (Bauman 1992) look pale. The permutability of technological information made possible by standardization and the interoperable character of information combine with the rapid diffusion of technologically extracted information out of information (that is, using specialized software) to strengthen the runaway and purpose-evading patterns of information growth. At the same time, these developments are intensifying the inherently ephemeral value of the information produced, thus increasing its disposability. This last observation brings us into the third of the three argumentative threads that weave the argument of the self-referential and escalating patterns of information growth.

3.5   The Disposability of Technological Information

The self-accruing processes of information growth analysed above are further accentuated by another highly elusive characteristic of information, that is, its short-lived and ephemeral character. In the contemporary technological world, the informativeness of information is subject to rapid depreciation and technological information essentially remains a highly disposable good (Borgmann 1999). This claim may *prima facie* seem counter-intuitive, even controversial, given the aura of persistence and durability conveyed by the technological nature of information and the sophisticated mechanisms for storing and retrieving data items. On the other hand, the huge amounts of information that are generated every day only to be relegated soon thereafter to the silent and withdrawn world of stored data provide evidence of the ephemeral and disposable character of information. Let's examine these issues in more detail.

As claimed in section 3.2, information as a semantic phenomenon must be distinguished both from the sign tokens by which it is carried and the wider concept of knowledge. Information is but the semantic content that crops up out of the

play of differences understood at the level of meaning as semantic distinctions. To be informative, however, information must
bring forward another difference, for the carrying over of
semantic distinctions that are already known does not qualify as
information. In this respect, information differs from cognition,
that is, the perception of the world on the basis of a complex web
of differences.[14] The value of information is ultimately tied to the
new semantic pieces which the differences it brings forward are
able to add to what is already there. It is worth repeating
Bateson's (1972) innovative claim that information is not simply
a difference but a difference that makes a difference. If information is therefore defined by its novelty and its value by its degree
of novelty, then it comes as no surprise that value depreciation
inheres in information, and is what a shadow is to an object that
casts it. Against such a background, disposability emerges as
intrinsic to information, for novelty by definition does not and
cannot last.

Information that transcends its short-lived character, retaining
its value over time, undergoes a significant change in status, for
it is no longer defined by its novelty. By virtue of acquiring a
permanence in the forms in which it is implicated in social
affairs, information ceases to be information, being transformed
to something different, that is, knowledge, memory or even
culture (Boyden 2003; Luhmann 2002). It is important to distinguish information and the processes to which it is tied from
these wider phenomena. For even though knowledge, memory
and culture are also changing with the passage of time they are
mostly defined by their capacity to preserve and reproduce the
old. Information differs radically in that respect. The contingent
and time-limited character of information,[15] perhaps indicative
of the spirit of the current age, makes it firmly oriented towards
the present (as opposed to the past) and its aberrant and evanescent qualities (Bauman 2000; Lyotard 1984; Virilio 2000).
Alternatively, information can lose its informativeness yet retain
its syntactic constitution, thereby retreating to data that can be
recycled into information under novel conditions that could lead

14. In this sense, cognition is always a re-cognition made possible by the
     insertion and assimilation of perceptual details into mental structures
     often referred to as cognitive schemes (see for example Neisser 1976;
     Weick 1979a, b).
15. See section 3.2 above.

to the reinterpretation of these data (Borgmann 1999; Esposito 2003).

The 'news' information carries is thus by necessity evanescent and subject to easy and rapid depreciation, a trend that is substantially enhanced rather than mitigated by the distinctive qualities of technological information analysed in the preceding sections. For this reason, information must be constantly renewed and updated to retain its informativeness, a condition that seems to be closely associated with the asserted self-propelling character of information growth and its runaway dynamics. Financial markets epitomize the short-lived character of information. While living an ephemeral life, differences in the form of price changes induce transactions across the globe only to be forgotten an instant later as new price changes invade the digitized circuits of technological information.

Updating is crucial to technological information and provides a strong indication of its imminent perishability. Far from being accidental, the need to update information is the outcome of the evanescent nature of information (as distinct from knowledge) and its firm orientation towards capturing the event-like character of minute life episodes. Examples abound all across the information landscape covered by technological information, for example, medical registers, taxation systems, accounting and financial systems, police archives, stock markets and so forth. Without up-to-date information, all these complex socio-technical structures run the danger of losing a significant portion of their value. Indeed, compared to paper-based forms of dealing with information, one of the most crucial innovations of technological information is its relatively smooth and constantly improving automated forms of updatability. In contrast to knowledge, information is not concerned with the essence and durability of things but rather with the shifting and surface amalgamations which things (and states) enter and dissolve. Knowledge may change and does change periodically, yet its relative permanence resists what we typically mean by updating. To use the previous terminology (see section 3.2), the value of information is closely tied to contingencies, to the contemporaneous and event-like character of states or processes which it may help illuminate and possibly control. But it too dilutes and evaporates along with the very events it tries to capture.

Paradoxical as it may seem, the disposable character of information is both what makes information useful and useless at the same time. Its usefulness is derived from its capacity to address the rapid array of contingencies that beset the present (as opposed to the past or future) of a world that is in a state of perpetual change. Information is needed to contemplate alternative courses of action, to act and respond in a timely way to prevailing conditions, and to evaluate outcomes in due course. At the same time, however, contingency and change also depreciate information rapidly, making it irrelevant or obsolete and, at times, even misleading or detrimental. Uselessness itself triggers further the generation of information as a means of recompensing its rapid depreciation. The disposable and ephemeral character of information thus necessitates the development of complex organizational and technical arrangements that ensure the continuing relevance and actuality of information through constant updating, thereby participating in the self-referential, self-accruing nature of information processes characteristic of the contemporary world.

Large and persisting information structures of this sort, though, in which data are stored over significant periods of time, may not be thought of as subject to depreciation, at least not in the same way as information that stems from or is related to events. Yet information infrastructures substantially strengthen the disposability of information by both expanding considerably the production of new data and shortening the life cycles by which new data are produced and become available. As suggested above, the value of information dilutes even in large structures if these are not constantly updated and upgraded. But constant updating of information and upgrading of the computer-based systems by which it is sustained inevitably result in the depreciation of the old information, as depicted in the preceding sections. In particular, the new elements that are added to existing information bases inevitably reframe the information contained within them, rendering obsolete some pieces of information and changing the value of others. In large-scale information structures, such a process tends to accelerate naturally, due to the enormous volume of incoming technological information and its rapid accumulation. Once again, the depreciation of the old information content may not necessarily imply that the syntactic, material expression of that content (data) is itself depreciated: it may still retain and even increase its value. The perception of the counter-intuitive and perhaps controversial character of the claim concerning the disposability of information is often the outcome of the inability to distinguish systematically between data and information.

In sum, disposability and depreciation are constitutive characteristics of information that find a clear manifestation in the quest for its continuous updating. Indeed, updating is both an expression of and at the same time a solution to the intrinsic information qualities of disposability and depreciation. These qualities are critically involved in the escalating pattern of information growth while providing an explanation of it. The pending dilution of information value drives a self-defeating yet inescapable game, resembling the effort to catch the wind, to compensate for the imminent evaporation of the advantages it offers. Paradoxical as it may seem, the more information that is produced, the greater the disposability of the available information. The cycle is virtuous or vicious, depending on the observer's perspective. Usefulness can rapidly dissolve into uselessness, which forms a precondition for the usefulness of subsequent information.[16]

16. The following passage from Knorr-Cetina and Bruegger's (2002: 915) study of foreign exchange markets, which they refer to as cambist markets, provides a good illustration of the ephemeral character of information and the processes it incites: 'The information contained in prices, for example, not only helps dealers make decisions but also stimulates deals. In other words, the information that arrives with price changes continually excites the system into further trading. Thus the speculative exuberance (Shiller 2000, p. 3) and the volatility that are characteristics of cambist markets (as opposed to producer markets or intermediary trading) appear to be intrinsically connected to the fast flow of information . . . We argue that market reality itself is knowledge generated, that is, has no existence independent from the informational presentation of the market on screen that is provided by news agencies, analysts and traders themselves.' This passage marvellously illuminates the transient ways information is involved in contemporary economic, organizational and institutional life. Yet Knorr-Cetina and Bruegger unfortunately fail to distinguish between the persisting and time-resistant character of knowledge and the short-lived, ephemeral nature of information, and hence fail to draw the implications of that distinction. What they refer to as knowledge mostly entails the electronic mediation of transient events which price shifts represent, or other financially relevant news that may impinge on currency changes. It is not by accident that a major channel for the dissemination of this information is news agencies like Reuters. Obviously such information is interpreted against a broader background of professional skills, knowledge of institutional relationships and the like yet the market as 'information presentation . . . on screen' is mostly the accomplishment of the transient character of electronically mediated

The disposable character of information adds a significant component of complexity to the institutional arrangements with which information processes are associated. Complexity in this sense is the product of the very constitution of information processes, their intrinsic relational nature and character, rather than simply the outcome of the multiplicity of components defining the information landscape and the increasing interconnectedness of systems and operations (Kallinikos 1996, 1998b). It is the very disposability of information and its steady production out of information that evade manipulation, planning and control in the ordinary sense of these words. It is not possible to chart in advance the pattern of information disposability. That it becomes obsolete and irrelevant is the outcome of the interaction between many factors, including the production of information, itself hardly predictable but crucial. While particular aspects of information processes may be amenable to control, in the sense of being successfully deployed to assist the accomplishment of particular tasks, intention increasingly dilutes in the greater ecology of processes, systems and operations sustaining the production of information in organizations and the contemporary world at large (March 1988, 1994; March and Olsen 1976).

3.6   Concluding Remarks

I have, in this chapter, put forth a number of ideas intended to shed some light on the current dynamics of information growth. Rather than being the outcome of deliberate planning and action, information growth defies subordination to a single purpose, developing in a self-referential and self-propelling fashion that I have sought to summarize in three major arguments. First, information has a dual value as a description of a reference domain and as a relationship such a description may have or come to develop to already available descriptions within that domain or across reference domains. An inevitable concomitant of this systemic or structural view of information is the intrinsic possibilities it provides for the production of information out of information. Secondly, standardization and the interoperable character of contemporary information infrastructures

information. Indeed, without that transience cambist markets would have been deprived of their *raison d'être*. See also the next chapter commenting on the relationship between meaning, agency and information.

vastly expand the permutability of information items and sources, and thus contribute considerably to the production of information out of information and the self-propelling, runaway dynamics underlying information processes and their growth. Thirdly, information growth dynamics are intimately connected with the perishable and disposable status of information. The informativeness of information is by definition a transitory accomplishment and its pending dilution of value drives its ceaseless updating and reproduction as a means for recompensing or rehabilitating such a value depreciation.

The vast amounts of information (often useless and meaningless) that are generated and stored every day are hard to justify by recourse to the information needs of individual or collective agents. The view that traces information generating processes back to the intentions or objectives of social agents is too innocent or ideal to account for the complex, ambiguous and, to a certain degree, meaningless processes and patterns of information growth. To be sure, part of the information currently generated in the various settings of contemporary institutional life may conform to such an ideal. Yet an increasing amount of current information is produced out of a matrix of technological and institutional relationships that cannot be accounted for by an agency-centric and ultimately instrumental (means–ends) analysis that puts at the heart of these processes a sovereign individual or collective subject. Contemporary, technologically-led processes of information generation develop out of the complex interplay of a variety of factors in which meaning may be just one. Information is often identified as useful only after the data by which it is carried have been produced, while new needs and usages of information develop as a result of the sheer availability of data and the techniques of data processing and manipulation. These comments may however demand further elaboration, given the semantic status of information. This is the subject of the next chapter.

4. Excursus on Meaning, Purpose and Information

4.1 Agency and Meaning

Is the account of information growth developed in the preceding chapter ruling out any substantial role which meaning and human purpose may play in the relative processes? After all, as distinct from sheer data, information is inherently meaningful. The processes, therefore, by which it is sought, generated and used should be tied to individual or collective agents and their pursuits. For particular aspects of life rendered as information emerge as meaningful only against the background of socially shared meanings and the practices which these sustain. This is a view that is encountered, in one form or another, across a variety of contributions on the subject (see for example Bowker and Star 1999; Brown and Duguid 2000; Orlikowski 2000). Is not then the proposed explanation of technological information and its growth dynamics in terms of self-referentiality an instance of what has come to be labelled technological determinism?

Surely, the explanation of information growth which I have put forth in the preceding chapter sits uncomfortably with a widespread sentiment encountered among laymen, policy makers and social scientists alike, and a concomitant belief according to which information should ultimately serve human and social needs, and be useful or meaningful only to the degree that it accomplishes these goals. Benign as it may be, such a belief amounts, however, to no more than an ideology. Agency-centric accounts of information management and growth are convenient and agreeable. They often reinforce the ideology of human-centrism that descends from romanticism and tranquillize the stirring anxiety that stems from the powerlessness people may feel vis-à-vis the huge and often incomprehensible information machine at work, which current technological processes epitomize. But they are too expedient to stand up to thorough critical scrutiny. Finding a purpose or an agent behind every social process or outcome is too simple an account of contemporary institutional life.

The three major explanatory arguments put forth in the preceding chapter suggest that even when starting meaningfully, as responses to the needs facing particular individuals, groups or organizations, technological information processes may and do end up quite differently. 'Intention is lost', to use March and Olsen's (1989: 14) poignant expression, as technological information processes sooner or later become caught up in the expanded circuits of digitized data that transform or drive them away from the objectives which may have initially motivated them (Ciborra 2000). In the preceding chapter, I have tried to present a variety of roles and functions which individual or collective objectives, and the meanings by which they are supported, play amidst these ambiguous and hardly controllable processes.

Institutional and social concerns, as reflected in the dominant semantics, assume an important role in supporting the established organizational and technological arrangements within which technological information processes take place. At aggregate levels, dominant meaning systems provide the institutionally and culturally anchored means, on the basis of which information is generated, selected and filtered, and constitute in this way a driving force in the patterns and direction of information growth (Borgmann 1999; Bowker and Star 1999; Dreyfus 2001). Shifts in prevailing concerns and orientations are also driving the developments of new structures for generating information regarding specific aspects of contemporary life (for example terrorism, environment, travel, insurance policies). In this process, new data sources are deliberately established, some of which are but combinations of old data sources and information items. Equally, less inclusive concerns are involved in the production of locally-based information growth patterns in accordance with the semantics that reflects the dominant meaning systems of particular groups and situated agents and their pursuits (Brown and Duguid 2000; Zuboff 1988).

The participation of meaning in the patterns of information growth seems reasonable and *prima facie* hard to deny. Yet, as I have been at pains to show, the involvement of meaning in information growth dynamics is part of a much larger and ambiguous game which agency-centric accounts of information growth often unduly simplify. In so doing, they downplay or even entirely bypass the crucial role played by a variety of non-agency-centric factors or processes characteristic of the complexity of the contemporary world. To begin with, meaning itself is complexly implicated in the constitution of social life. Meaning is a recalcitrant human ally. Collective meaning systems do not belong to anyone, often defining and constituting particular forms of agency and subjectivity.[1] While defining the agendas of individuals and organizations, encompassing meaning systems of this sort do develop and change through action but seldom because of particular initiatives. Change in meaning systems is, as a rule, the outcome of cumulative processes taking place over larger time spans and involving an intricate game of intended goals, unintended consequences, errors, omissions, emergent forces and the like. Rather than being a transcendental precondition of information processes, meaning is implicated in these processes and is itself changing under the influence of a variety of forces over which social agents may have little control or discretion.

The importance in particular of haphazard or emerging events, which I have underscored in various ways in the proposed explanation of technological information growth, becomes even more crucial in an interconnected and complex world, whose strings are pulled by a multitude of dispersed agents and initiatives. Elements of this game are certainly predictable and perhaps accountable in terms of human motives or situated pursuits, but the overall, aggregate outcome is not. Most of the technological innovations that have taken place over the past few decades would have been hard to imagine, let alone to predict, a few decades ago. Social practices and local pursuits are essential in setting into motion and perhaps shaping partic-

---

1.   I may appear here to invoke the Durkheimian ghost whereby individuals or even social groups are considered as no more than the 'site of socialization', as Margaret Archer (2002) has aptly formulated it, leaving little or no room for individuation or the development of local responses. The relationship between the individual and society represents a highly intricate and persisting issue in social theory which cannot be dealt with here (see Douglas 1986; Giddens 1991; Heller 1999). What I would however like to suggest in this context is that individual or local responses are insufficient to understand and account for such complex and aggregate socio-technical dynamics occasioned by contemporary technological processes.

ular technical innovations but, again, they cannot explain the aggregate pattern of these innovations. In the preceding chapter, I have tried to lay bare these processes by reference to a variety of contradictions and mutual implications with which techno-logical information processes are associated.

The relevance and explanatory power of agency-centric accounts of information growth emerge too as severely limited against the background of the self-reinforcing character of social structures (Klein and Kleinman 2002). Institutional relation-ships, organizational arrangements, established mechanisms and procedures are often involved in the reproduction of the matrix of relationships which they support without immediate reference to meaning or purpose. Some of these characteristics are further reinforced by the ceremonial or ritualistic character of institutionally-anchored action. Most crucially, perhaps, tech-nological and institutional processes entail path-dependent patterns of development that reinforce past choices in ways that are hardly reversible or negotiable in the short run (Arthur 1994; Hanseth 2000; Hanseth and Braa 2000), occasionally giving rise to a self-propelling runaway dynamic (Giddens 1990; Hanseth *et al.* 2001). Separately or in concert, these factors expose the restrictive character of agency-centric explanations of contem-porary information growth and limit their plausibility (Introna 1977).

Aggregate information growth patterns are therefore not reducible to human purpose in any straightforward manner, even though meaning and purpose are involved in one way or another in shaping parts of this intricate socio-technical land-scape. Meaning is indispensable in information processes, in the sense of providing the generative matrix out of which distinc-tions arise and relevancies and motives are established[2] but much less in the sense of action capable of subsuming the world under its wings. To be sure, to the degree that meaning is inher-ently conservative (that is, tending to reproduce itself), a group's or a community's dominant significations act as both a guide and a stabilizing force for information growth. Only a limited set of combinatorial possibilities is explored, that is, those whose purpose emerges in one way or another against the background of the predominant understandings. However, the account of

2. See section 3.2 in the preceding chapter on conceptual clarifications and definitions.

information growth in terms of the conservative character of meaning is concerned with sameness rather than difference, stability rather than change; a concern that becomes too much of a burden, given the explosive growth of information over the last few decades. It also attributes a dependent or derivative status to information growth, viewing it as the outcome of a community's struggle to manage its affairs in accordance with those goals, priorities and interests that derive from the prevailing meaning systems.

The account of information growth dynamics I have put forth suggests a different interpretation, even though it does not rule out the participation of meaning in that dynamic. In the process I have sought to describe in the preceding chapter, meaning is no more than a supplement, or, to use a figurative language, a satellite whose orbit is forever tied to the planet (self-reference, permutability, disposability) around which it keeps turning. Meaning, purpose and agency are surely participants yet, as already suggested, in the much larger game which contemporary technologically-based information processes exemplify they are neither the point of departure nor the final destination to which these processes aim. While particular information processes may be predictable and explainable as meaningful responses to particular problems, the overall growth pattern of information processes taking place at aggregate levels is a considerably emergent outcome, seldom reducible to the goals of particular agents. The philosophical underpinnings of this partly uncontrollable growth pattern of information are provided by the non-foundational understanding of information as difference that makes a difference (Bateson 1972), as described in the preceding chapter.[3]

In technologically-based information processes, correlations of data items within and across sources are bound to occur despite appearing meaningless in the first place. Given the spectacular and deep involvement of technology in institutional affairs, many such correlations will increasingly be generated by software-run machines, on the basis of predominantly syntactic similarities, as the examples of search engines and profiling techniques mentioned earlier suggest. Some of these combinations may be found meaningful *a posteriori*, thereby reversing the aforementioned, traditional understanding whereby meaning

3.   See section 3.3 in the preceding chapter.

engulfs and produces information. In other cases, in which human participation assumes more immediate forms, combinations or correlations of data items may suggest meanings (purposes) that would never have emerged without the complicity, as it were, of the technical availability of these combinations. Furthermore, the sheer availability and technical feasibility of arriving at new combinations which current technology enables may provide the impetus or the incentives for playfully exploring information and information rules without immediate purpose.[4]

The indirect involvement of meaning in the processes of information growth is further illustrated by the aforementioned claim of the intrinsically disposable status of information. Disposability, it has been claimed, drives the need of information generation as a means for recompensing or rehabilitating the rapid dilution of the value of information. Information disposability suggests that it may be the lack of meaning rather than meaning itself that drives the generation of information and the dynamics of its growth. The disposable status of information suggests that meaning is implicated (as lack) in the patterns of information growth but not in the directive and straightforward way traditional, agency-centric accounts of information often imply. Meaning participates in the processes of information generation and growth in indirect and oblique ways, often being just an outcome, although crucially a shifting and temporary one, rather than the ultimate matrix out of which information is born.

4.2   Beyond Information

The limits of information growth are neither to be found in the inherent meaninglessness of data nor in the ways in which social agents are able to bend, wittingly or unwittingly, information processes to serve their purposes. If there are any limits to which informatization is subject, then these should be explored with reference to those aspects of the world (material,

---

4.   A significant part of open-source produced software, I suggest, contains strong elements of such playful explorations in which the distinction between means (the technology) and ends (the code produced) collapses, making meaning emerge concurrently with the explorative behaviour or even *a posteriori* (Iannacci 2005).

social and institutional) that resist yielding to their rendition as
information. As Brown and Duguid (2000: 4) cogently remark
'(g)enerations of confident videophones, conferencing tools, and
technologies for tele-presence are still far from capturing the
essence of a firm handshake or a straight look in the eye'. Perhaps,
someday they will. The developmental trajectory of computational
technologies attests to their growing ability to conquer new
domains of the real with a steadily improving quality in the means
and the outcomes of technological mediation (Hayles 2005).

The expansion and qualitative improvement of technology
notwithstanding, there are reasons to believe that a variety of
aspects of physical and social life exist that will never entirely
yield to their transformation to information. Those aspects of
nature, intimacy or public life that resist informatization will
come to represent the blind spot of technological information,
and the ultimate limit to its capacity to govern human and social
relationships. By contrast, those domains of the real that become
informatized are, sooner or later, bound to be caught in the digitized vortex of technological information along those lines
analysed in the preceding chapter. What sort of balance will
come to be established between the two spheres (information
and reality) is difficult to predict and is essentially outside the
scope of the present commentary. Information will certainly
grow but would such a development take place at the expense of
real reality? Is the relationship between the two domains to be
gauged in terms of substitutability or does a mutual support and
reinforcement exist?

Woolgar (2002) has suggested that the expansion of informatized versions of life is bound to create a growing need to
support the immateriality of the virtual and its fragility with the
crutches of real life. He posited that the more the virtual
expands, the more the real becomes necessary; a relationship
that is not discordant with the epistemic comments I supplied in
the preceding chapter with respect to information/signs and
reality (see also Borgmann 1999: ch. 14, 15). I neither wish nor am
I able to deal with these highly intricate issues here. I refer to
these in order to highlight that the limits of information are to be
sought beyond information in the ambiguous, antithetical and
mutually supportive relationship which it entertains to whatever information is not (Introna 1997). Such a project, in turn,
necessitates the displacement of the construct of the social agent
located at the centre of things and the understanding of socio-

technical processes in terms that transcend agency-centric explanations (Heidegger 1977).[5]

4.3   Implications

The account of information growth advanced in this and the preceding chapter suggests that any attempt to control information growth processes is subject to powerful limits, and may even produce unanticipated and unwanted consequences. This is, in itself, a detracting proposition that may appear to rule out the possibility of drawing practical implications based on the analysis undertaken in these two chapters. If, after all, information processes evade human control, then the effort to analyse them in order to improve the quality of human decisions and the operations which these processes sustain would seem rather futile. Yet the understanding of information growth advanced here does have some practical implications, the most important of which, I dare to propose, is the deep awareness it helps bring about of the intricate web of processes and forces out of which information grows.

The realization of the intricacies of information growth dynamics may become an important factor in dissipating a number of false expectations that lie at the heart of many practical problems and disappointments with respect to what particular technological initiatives can accomplish. The failure of many large-scale systems to deliver their promise is not solely the result of the misunderstanding of the very conditions under which they are implemented and the inadequate adaptation of information packages to these conditions. Such failure is not an issue that can be explained exhaustively in terms of proper methods and procedures of implementation, or even in terms of a more adequate design of new technologies that the bitter

---

5.   Some may find these comments to be bordering the conception of socio-technical change in terms reminiscent of Actor-Network Theory (ANT). There may undeniably be a number of common points. I have found, however, that the construct of the 'actant' is too caught up in an agency-morphic preconception of social processes. I also consider the a-historical nature of ANT and the unwillingness of its proponents to look beyond the micro-foundations of the 'network' towards aggregate societal processes taking place in larger time frames too much of a restriction. See for example Kallinikos (2004c) and Misa *et al.* (2003). For a more thorough critique of ANT and information see Klaus (2004).

lessons of experience are supposed to bring back to the software laboratory.[6] To some degree such a failure is endemic and the high rate of betrayed expectations following the implementation of large-scale systems seems to provide evidence of this. The awareness therefore that the present analysis may bring can help cultivate a series of attitudes and predispositions vis-à-vis the relative processes that are underlain by care, humility and consideration in dealing with information along the lines described by Ciborra and his associates (Ciborra 2000, 2002).[7]

Following the analysis of information growth put forth here, other implications include those associated with the proactive design of social systems in ways that may create instrumental enclosures of the types analysed in Chapter 2. Even though wider information growth processes can neither be understood in terms of individual or collective initiatives nor fully be controlled by locally-embedded actors, particular zones of this complex aggregate may be subject to some control and deliberation. As Perrow (1984) has suggested, the loose coupling of information systems and processes may be a key strategy to follow whenever the impact of processes within and across systems is non-linear and the understanding or control of cause–effect relationships is partial. Functional simplification and closure, or the relative independence of one system from another, may therefore emerge as viable controlling strategies. In fact, modular information architectures embody that strategy to a certain

6. The complex web of self-propelling patterns into which information processes are embedded suggests that key stages in the development and design of particular systems like those of 'user requirements' may be inadequate to capture the complexity and ambiguous character of change underlying the conditions under which many groups of users operate. The account of information growth I have offered in this volume goes far beyond the rethinking of what is called the traditional Systems Development Life Cycle (that is, analysis, requirements, coding). Changing 'user requirements' are, to a significant degree, the outcome of new information systems producing perpetually new information and diffusing new skills and operating procedures for dealing with information within and across organizations. No matter how successfully a system 'copies' the realities of the contexts which it is supposed to address, that reality is going to look different after the introduction of that system.

7. These ideas bear an affinity to Vattimo's (1989) outline of weak thinking as a way of rehabilitating humanity's declining ability to shape its condition. Lyotard (1991) too has described a similar attitude for dealing with meaning evaporation in the contemporary technological world.

degree. As I have been at pains to show in this and the two preceding chapters however, loose coupling as a strategy is at odds, at least partly, with the overall project of interconnectedness and interoperability that seems to be underlying the current development of information systems, large-scale information infrastructures and the internet.

The arguments developed in this volume and more specifically in the preceding chapter make clear the lack of an adequate theoretical understanding of information growth dynamics that could support a consistent effort to intervene in these processes. What has been proposed here can be no more than the point of departure for developing a theory of information growth dynamics in a connected world (Kallinikos 2005). Much more remains to be done in that direction. It is unfortunate that with few exceptions (see for example Kling 1996), social theorists do not give current information growth dynamics the attention it deserves, despite the frequent recognition of its importance manifested, among other things, in terms like 'information society' and 'information age'. When this occasionally occurs (for example, Hylland-Eriksen 2001; Lash 2001, 2002; Virilio 2000) the degree of generality is too high to be able to reflect the distinctive character of the contemporary processes of information growth. Information systems scholars, on the other hand, have traditionally been preoccupied with the design and implementation of individual systems, no matter how large and important these may have been.

The intermediate zone where information systems and information processes encounter wider societal concerns has therefore remained relatively underdeveloped. The preceding chapter and to a certain degree this one have sought to make a contribution in this respect. The major claims they have advanced arguably constitute a point of departure for the study of information processes that develop beyond the boundaries of particular systems and organizations. It is obvious that the developments analysed here cannot but have far-reaching implications for the constitution of formal organizations as bounded, hierarchical systems and the wider instrumental environment within which particular groups and organizations operate. Having prepared the groundwork, let me now return to the in-depth consideration of networks and the economic and organizational challenges they pose to the established institutional order.

5. Networks Revisited

5.1 Introduction

Networks have recently attracted a great deal of scholarly attention which may conceal the fact that research on networks has been around for quite a while. Indeed, the relevant literature is both massive and fragmented and, for that reason, hardly surveyable. There is an economic literature on networks stemming from the tradition of industrial organization (Eccles 1981; Storper 1989, 1993) and one that originates in institutional economics (Arrow 1974; Coase 1937; North 1981; Williamson 1975, 1981). There exists too a rather comprehensive but disparate sociological literature on networks (Burt 1982; Cook and Whitmeyer 1992; Fukuyama 1997; Sassen 2001; White 1981, 2002), itself a reflection of the conceptual diversity of sociology. Key contributions across these literatures have been brought to bear upon related issues in the narrower fields of organization theory (Aldrich 1979; Grandori and Soda 1995; Kallinikos 1995; Powell 1990) and industrial marketing (Håkansson 1982; Hägg and Johanson 1982) and have yielded a substantial body of research on networks. The novel popularity which research on networks has lately acquired (Castells 1996, 2000, 2001; DeSanctis and Monge 1999; Thompson 2003, 2004; Wellman and Haythornthwaite 2002) continues a tradition that goes back several decades. There is, no doubt, considerable overlap between all these literatures but also crucial differences regarding the understanding of the term, the role it plays within contemporary economy and society, and the structural mechanisms and socioeconomic dynamics with which it is associated.

The diversity and the different paradigmatic roots underlying this literature make the effort to summarize it almost futile. And yet, there are zones of convergence that partly explain the migration of the term *network* across disciplines and its, real or imagined, explanatory power. One such zone is demarcated by the very (pre-)understanding of networks as a coordinative arrangement, alternative or complementary to those of formal organizations and of markets (Fukuyama 1997; Knorr-Cetina and Bruegger 2002; Powell 1990; Rifkin 2000). In this respect, networks are seen as governance mechanisms that occasionally challenge, and other times complement, both the bounded and the hierarchical constitution of formal organizations (that is, private firms and public agencies) and the spot, price-mediated exchanges commonly associated with markets (see for example Kallinikos 1995). Even though the preconception of networks as an alternative coordinative arrangement to formal organizations and markets has itself been predicated on widely varying assumptions, it has nonetheless helped constitute a cross-disciplinary terrain within which the term has become a kind of common currency. The contradistinction of networks to markets and formal organizations offers, I suggest, a point of departure for dealing with the versatility of the term noted in the introductory chapter. For, in being juxtaposed to markets and formal organizations, networks are predominantly conceived as instrumental, performative arrangements or practices to be distinguished from other social forms such as groups or community networks.[1] Much more remains to be done in this direction though, and I will put forth several suggestions as the chapter unfolds.

The recent popularity of networks owes much to or is, in any case, related to the economic and instrumental habitat which the information growth analysed earlier in this volume tends to establish. The economic and managerial practices associated with networks could be interpreted as a key manifestation of the processes through which the composite and rapidly growing domain of information increasingly engulfs the operations of organizations, and redefines the terms under which the production and distribution of goods and services occurs. Information management has historically been a supplementary group of operations that formed part of the wider group of non-production functions in organizations; it has thus been conditioned by the exigencies of supporting and managing the core processes of

1. Such a conception of networks therefore excludes other contemporary social contexts which, due to the significance of the internet or other computer-based networks, have been described as involving a variety of networking activities, that is, electronic communities, internet-based social networks and the like (for example, DiMaggio *et al.* 2001; Steinmueller 2002; Venkatesh 2003; Wellman and Haythornthwaite 2002).

producing and distributing goods and services. However, the significance that information has assumed over the last few decades has conferred these functions with novel qualities, increasingly immersing information processes in a wider ecology of practices that transgress, in a variety of ways, organizational boundaries and the immediate control of managerial hierarchy.

As shown, mainly in Chapter 3, information processes in particular settings intertwine with a variety of wider economic, technological and institutional initiatives. This way, information is generated, processed, stored and communicated to form progressively a major and, most crucially, continuously expanding trans-organizational domain of data and messages. A major implication of the growing instrumental entanglement of information processes has been the progressive orientation of key management and control functions in organizations away from the monitoring of the bounded and local character of core throughput processes. These developments ride on and at the same time reinforce a long-wave change that has been manifested by the growing significance which non-production functions, like marketing and finance, have progressively acquired in organizations over the course of the twentieth century (Fligstein 1990). Currently, the successful performance of marketing, and to an even greater extent of finance, significantly depend on the technological control and distribution of information over zones that extend far beyond the instrumental enclosures traditionally associated with the bounded and hierarchical organization.

Taken together these developments point to the wider context of technological, organizational and economic changes with which networks are associated. In what follows, I briefly review some widespread claims that associate information and communication technologies with patterns of interaction and work and a variety of practices that are said to be conducive to the structural arrangement of the network. In so doing I seek to lay bare and occasionally question a few key assumptions on which these claims are predicated. Next, I endeavour to develop an alternative explanation of networks that is closely associated with the contemporary growth dynamic of information and the technologies by which it is sustained and given momentum. As suggested several times, informatization contributes to the decomposability of a growing number of operations and resources once they have been rendered as information. The resulting mobility makes it possible to lift such operations out of particular contexts and transfer, reshuffle and recombine them, often on a global scale. At the same time, the interlocking of information derived from a larger infospace (suppliers, consumers, market dynamics and so on) alters the balance of relevancies and the perception of opportunities, and shifts the focus away from concern with predominantly local contingencies. These developments expose some of the limitations of formal organizations instrumented and run as bounded and hierarchical entities, and are related to their disaggregation and the diffusion of networks as alternative coordinative arrangements. In this respect, technological information growth reshapes important conditions under which the production of goods and services takes place.

5.2   Information, Electronic Transactivity and Networks

I have, in the previous chapters, considered the role that computer-based technologies of information and communication, as an overarching technological paradigm, have been playing in promoting new modes of instrumental involvement and control. Before I draw the implications of that analysis further, it would be appropriate to consider a bit more closely a predominantly empirical literature that, over the last two decades, has sought to document the organizational implications of the diffusion of information and communication technologies and the internet. In what follows I summarize, rather indicatively, some of the findings from that literature without any claims to representativeness. My purpose is one of integrating some of the insights of that literature into the major argument that I am about to advance. In so doing, I endeavour to show the way the present chapter, and the volume in its entirety, deviate from established ways of conceiving the restructuring role of information, and the technologies by which information processing and communication are supported. I subsume that literature review under three blocks that take up successively: the structural implications of computer-based technology in organizations; its role in promoting new distributed modes of work; and the forms by which it is implicated in outsourcing informatized tasks and services as an instance of the above-mentioned dissolvability of organizational operations.

To begin with, computer-based technologies of information and communication have commonly been associated with important changes in the conditions under which the production of goods and services takes place, as suggested in the first part of Chapter 2. The gradual yet far-reaching automation of materially-based processes and administrative tasks has resulted in the redefinition or reparsing of a growing number of organizational operations, and the emergence and diffusion of a variety of novel tasks (DiMaggio *et al.* 2001; Kling 1996; Sinha and Van de Ven 2005; Zuboff 1988). One major implication of these developments has been the rising significance of information in terms of its involvement in the planning, execution and monitoring of organizational operations (Zuboff 1988). Coupled with new, efficient and less costly modes of communicating across functional divisions, hierarchical levels and separate sites, the significance both of information and of the changes it has induced in the task infrastructure of organizations has exerted strong pressures upon the governance mechanisms and the structural morphology of organizations (that is, role systems, hierarchical levels, span of control, standard operating procedures and so on) towards administrative simplification, flatter hierarchies and leaner processes (for example, DiMaggio *et al.* 2001; Fulk and DeSanctis 1995; Malone 2004; Nohria and Buckley 1994; Sinha and Van de Ven 2005).

Rather than being solely reflected in the internal restructuring of organizations, the growing involvement of information and communication technologies has also weakened the crucial function of organizational boundaries and the role they have traditionally assumed in the overall controlling strategies of bounded and hierarchical systems. In many instances in which computer-based technologies have been heavily involved in organizations, the redefinition and restructuring of many organizational tasks has made necessary their execution under conditions entailing extensive transactions and lateral liaisons with other actors or constituencies in an organization's environment (Knorr-Cetina and Bruegger 2002; Sinha and Van de Ven 2005; Starkey *et al.* 1999). Taken together, these developments have been associated with the emergence of organizational practices or arrangements and modes of interaction that have either transformed the bounded and hierarchical character of formal organizations or given rise to alternative organizational forms, of which the network is a major instance (Castells 1996, 2000, 2001; DeSanctis and Monge 1999).

Some of these relationships have been supported by empirical evidence, yet the overall empirical picture emerges as much more complicated (Brown and Duguid 2000). Centralization and decentralization, local autonomy and central control systems, disaggregation and empire building mix in various ways that resist easy generalization (Ahuja and Carley 1999; Sassen 2001; Zuboff 1988). Despite that, the view that contemporary technologies of information and communication are a major agent of decentralization, boundary crossing and networking has continued to enjoy widespread currency (Castells 2001; Malone 2004; Mowshowitz 2002). The understanding of information and communication technologies as a causal force behind the emergence of networks is, to a certain degree, justifiable against the background of the dense information arteries they provide across systems, regions and nations. Yet messages and decisions should be distinguished from the sheer flow of data along the computer-supported communication networks. After all, organizational arrangements are not data flows.

Second, information and communication technologies and the internet have been associated with the advent and diffusion of work methods which are commonly referred to as distributed. As distinct from the implications mentioned above, distributed forms of work challenge traditional work practices from a rather different route, one that involves weakening the significance that location has traditionally assumed as a key organizing platform and instrument of control (DeSanctis and Monge 1999; Hinds and Mortensen 2005; Knorr-Cetina and Bruegger 2002; Schmidt and Bannon 1992; Sinha and Van de Ven 2005; Sproull and Kiesler 1991; Wellman *et al.* 1996). Any primacy which location has historically acquired as the blueprint for carrying out work, partly derives from the rich communicative context of face-to-face interaction and the inescapable situatedness of traditional forms of oral communication (Zuboff 1988). Yet site organization of work has also been closely associated with the wider mechanisms of surveillance and control that spatio-temporal inclusion makes possible (Deleuze 1995; Thompson and Alvesson 2005; Zuboff 1988).[2]

In this respect, and via its own route, distributed work seems to challenge established work practices and the structural arrangements that have traditionally accommodated them.

2. For more details see Chapter 2.

Distributed work undermines, or at least weakens, the importance of hierarchical mechanisms of control based on proximity, supervision and normative compliance; the latter is an intrinsic attribute and accompaniment to group participation. It further accentuates the limits of hierarchy and crucially makes necessary the coordination of work participants through multiple instant feedback loops that defy, or render unsustainable, cumbersome hierarchical mediation (Sproull and Kiesler 1991; Wellman *et al.* 1996). In yet another way, distributed work provides the basis for project-based temporary work arrangements that limit the efficacy of standard, location-bound and hierarchical control structures (Castells 1996, 2000, 2001; Malone 2004; Sproull and Kiesler 1991). Again and despite the apparently reasonable character of these claims, empirical evidence on the subject is contradictory (Ahuja and Carley 1999; DiMaggio *et al.* 2001). Distributed work is not an exercise in brotherhood; it often takes place under conditions of strong individual competition and distrust that significantly moderate whatever impact information and communication technologies may have in promoting shared and open practices (Orlikowski 1996, 2000). In addition, distributed work and the networks it may be associated with are framed by the prevailing stratified social topology of organizations, and the ways hierarchy and the interests it embodies seek to accommodate these technological developments (Ekbia and Kling 2005; Zuboff 1988; Sassen 2001).

Third, information and communication technologies and the internet make available a technological platform for the development of the practice of outsourcing and subcontracting in comprehensive and cost-efficient ways. In so doing, they provide novel incentives for reframing the logic upon which boundedness, location and hierarchy as major and constitutive organizational principles have been predicated (Castells 2001; Davidow and Malone 1992; Malone and Laubacher 1998; Rifkin 2000). Subcontracting has always involved the key question of what to produce in-house versus what to acquire from the market. Such a question has been addressed within the framework of constraints imposed by the stage of technological development, and the prevailing division of labour and the institutional forms accommodating it. In this respect, outsourcing mediated by the new technologies of information and communication substantially enlarges the scope of what is possible by reducing coordination costs and making technically feasible the polyvalent planning, communication and control of cross-site and cross-organizational operations (Malone 2004; Rifkin 2000).

Falling communication costs and the broader spectrum of activities that can be coordinated through current forms of computer-mediated interaction only partly explain the spread of global practices of sourcing. Before they become externalized or procured in the global market, services or resources have to become mobile and transferable across settings. The mobility of many services is contingent upon the dissolvability of context-embedded operations that informatization confers and the standardization of technologies (software and hardware) involved in this process. Informatization that rides on software and hardware standardization increases the interoperability of the informatized functions and tasks and, provided that these are adequately modularized and packaged, also raises their transferability across contexts. As the case of finance makes clear, modularization and mobility are crucial preconditions for the tradability or exchangeability of many services and operations, often on a global scale (Sassen 2001). Under these conditions, computer-sustained outsourcing of services becomes a key strategy for reshuffling and recombining detachable and modularized operations between and among organizations. The formation of network arrangements becomes, in this sense, an important means for gaining advantage from the associated economies of experience and specialization (Wigand *et al.* 1997; Sassen 2001; Sinha and Van de Ven 2005). This is a key argument to which I return soon.

Despite the reasonable character of the claims portraying information and communication technologies as a major agent of organizational change, the empirical evidence, as already indicated, is contradictory and far from conclusive (Brown and Duguid 2000; Kelly 1998; Kling 1996). The possibilities that are associated with technologically-induced social change seem to be inescapably mediated by the nexus of power, the institutional relationships to which power is associated and other cultural or social forms that embody the cumulative effects of experience and social learning (Brown and Duguid 2000; Douglas 1986; Fligstein 2001; Zuboff and Maxmin 2003). Furthermore, the tangle formed by these factors is frequently punctuated by contingencies of various sorts that make the connection between means and ends an insecure accomplishment. Separately, or in concert, these factors are involved in the drift away from the preconceived goals that particular technologies and systems are claimed to serve (Ciborra 2000), a condition that further complicates the straightforward attribution to technology of a causal status tied to particular organizational outcomes. I sought to account for some of these processes in the preceding two chapters by recourse to the self-referential, self-induced character of the current information growth dynamics.

The complex and ambiguous nature of social and economic change is conspicuously shown in the case of networks by the institutional nexus of relationships (for example, property rights, employment contracts and forms of legal accountability) that heavily condition the diffusion of networks (Fligstein 2001). An appreciation of the organizational developments under way must therefore be situated within the established legal-institutional framework of the typical modern social order. Placed within such a wider socio-historical context, formal organization emerges not simply as an administrative or production apparatus but crucially as a solid or persistent social form: an institution for constructing public accountability and governing social relations in the workplace in a formal and lawful manner that is concordant with the overall spirit of democratic societies. The appreciation of the social and institutional complexity which formal organization epitomizes inevitably begs the question concerning the institutional status of networks, and the ways networks challenge formal organizations not simply as administrative/instrumental arrangements but as a key institutional form in modernity. The literature on these matters has been mostly silent, and when not silent rather unclear (Castells 2000, 2001; DiMaggio 2001; Heckscher and Donnellon 1994; Malone 2004; Steinmueller 2002). I return to this subject in the next two chapters, after I develop an interpretation of networks that ties their diffusion to the instrumental significance of technological information.

5.3 Information as a Habitat

Any straightforward causal connection between information and communication technologies and the organizational arrangements they are claimed to engender should be rejected as inadequate for capturing the dynamics of social and organizational change. The impact of technology on social forms is heavily shaped by the social, cultural and institutional relations into which the technology is embedded. However, as meaningful as it is, such a claim does not get very far in charting the organizational and institutional implications of current technological developments. I have tried to show in the preceding chapters that technology matters, even though its social and organizational significance should not be gauged in terms of straightforward cause–effect relationships. In this respect, the current research on information and communication technologies, work and organizational forms summarized above does have the potential of contributing to a better appreciation of the relevant issues, but only if the empirical findings it has produced are adequately framed and interpreted.

A key implication, I suggest, emerging from the three strands of literature summarized above, is that the diffusion of technological information is involved in the remaking of the underlying infrastructural conditions that have accommodated the dominant structural and interaction arrangements within organizations (Ciborra 1997; Lilley *et al.* 2004). The fuller accommodation of this implication, however, makes it necessary to place the remaking of the task infrastructure of organizations, consequent upon informatization, within the theoretical context presented in Chapters 2 and 3. In what follows I make an effort to synthesize these chapters and present the changing architecture of infrastructural conditions established by the growing importance of the technological paradigm of computation, and the making of information into a major means for conceiving, instrumenting and controlling organizational operations.

It is quite common to associate whatever implications computer-based technologies may have for organizations with the changing communication and interaction patterns they enable. However, crucial as they may be, shifts in modes of communicating and interacting are second-order effects that presuppose the rendition of reality at the level of information. The far-reaching organizational implications of the technological paradigm of computation should be sought in its capacity to capture a growing range of operations into the medium of information, and to reconstitute these operations as elaborate series of automated rules and procedures for processing data. The rendition of the task infrastructure of organizations as information is, by necessity, predicated on the meticulous and relentless analytical parsing and decomposition of all those tasks and operations that become informatized. Given the computational constitution of computer-based technology and the nature of programming, there is no other way to proceed to coding and informatization. Task conditions and relationships must be represented as a series of discrete operations, dissolved into elementary steps and recomposed into larger sequences by means of the rules and procedures that constitute the essence of programming.[3]

Understood as cognitive decomposition and recomposition, informatization dissolves the depths (the underlying elementary micro-structure) and compound nature of organizational operations. It does so in an analogous fashion to the informatized representation decomposing the depth of the earth through soil or mineral decomposition, or recapturing its extension through geographical information systems (Borgmann 1999; Cooper 1991; Kallinikos 1996). The microscopic nature of computation casts its analytical gaze far behind the observable character of objects and social processes. Computation pierces deep into organizational reality, dissolves it into its elementary 'particles' and reconstitutes it as information and combinations of information items. In this way, an essential part of organizational conditions that eluded observability and inspection is rendered visible and, most crucially, pliable and manipulable. It comes, therefore, as no surprise that an inevitable consequence of comprehensive informatization has been the growing dissolvability of the dense fabric of the composite and context-embedded nature of many organizational operations (Borgmann 1999; Kallinikos 1996; Zuboff 1988). Tasks that were previously considered to be indissoluble units or, in any case, functionally interdependent with other tasks (for example, accounting, inventory management, production operations, financial management) have been able to be dissolved and recomposed as informatized modules or services essentially supported by a variety of information packages. The diffusion of service outsourcing[4] is just a specific expression of the loosening task interdependencies that comprehensive informatization brings about, and the changing division of labour that is resulting from these developments.

The decomposability of organizational tasks combines with

3. For more details see Chapters 2 and 3.
4. See Gartner group's recent report on so-called business process outsourcing, Gartner (2004).

the heightened control of cross-context transactions, the lowering costs of communication and the growing interoperability of computer-based systems and technologies to increase the transferability of informatized operations across settings. An important organizational consequence of these developments has been the technical possibility of separating the inescapable context-embedded and materially-conditioned character of the production of goods and services from other operations of a more strategic or crucial nature. Examples of this last are provided by specialized, knowledge-intensive services (producer services) or the design, availability and monitoring of the global distribution of goods and services (Sassen 2001). Under these conditions, the combinability of resources and activities across space and time greatly expands and the opportunities for pursuing such combinations profitably or efficiently become substantially enlarged. Now such a separation could be thought of as intrinsic to the deepening division of labour characteristic of capitalist production and the economies of specialization it helps generate. Indeed, historically, the significance that (producer) services have acquired in the information age could be understood in this way (Bell 1976; Castells 1996; Webster 2002). There is little doubt that economies of specialization are inextricably implicated in the dissolvability of organizational operations and the wider organizational implications that are usually associated with disaggregation and vertical disintegration (Greenfield 1996; Sassen 2001; Storper 1989, 1993). Yet specialization in many knowledge-intensive services is complexly intertwined with information management and the efficiency and lower cost of cross-boundary transactions which information and communication technologies enable.

The dissolvability of the composite texture of functionally interwoven operations brought about by informatization, transcends those effects commonly associated with specialization (Kallinikos 2004a; Mowshowitz 2002). Informatized dissolvability does not simply improve performance, as the result of the formation of specialized skills and better organizational practices; it is also involved, as I demonstrate over the next few pages, in the redefinition of some of the premises upon which economic and organizational action are predicated. This is due to the joint outcome of the deepening division of labour and a new architecture of control which technological information and communication enable. Decomposability and specialization are, no doubt, related to one another. Specialization by definition springs from a wider context of skills and technologies, entailing a narrower profile of skills and consequently often performing more efficiently. In this sense, the dissolvable or decomposable character of organizational operations that results from their growing informatization could be seen as both the outcome of specialization and a precondition for the emergence of further specialization gains.

Nevertheless, the effects that information growth may have on specialization do not exhaust its impact; it also has wider implications that reframe key premises upon which formal organizing has been predicated. The importance, I suggest, which information and information management assume in the current age is better appreciated against the background of the current dynamics underlying the spectacular growth of technological information analysed in Chapter 3. Such a dynamic reflects the confluence of several developments, a key manifestation of which is the expanding interoperability of available information sources and the technological systems by which they are sustained. The interoperable character of technological information is itself implicated in the self-referential generation of information out of information through the very juxtaposition, reshuffling, recycling and recombination of information items within and across the interoperable information sources and systems.

A few crucial, though evasive, organizational implications develop at this juncture. The self-referential information growth drives the rendition of economic operations at the level of information progressively away from the realities of production in particular organizational settings. Data and information drawn from customer monitoring, market dynamics, financial trends, supply chain integration and other sources regularly impinge upon and intersect with the layout and management of core operations, transforming their bounded and functionally simplified character. Informatization does not simply copy the contingencies in which these operations are embedded. It also becomes increasingly entangled with other information sources beyond the boundaries of particular settings, as it seeks to accommodate or gain advantage from available information that is circulating in a far larger infospace. In this sense, information growth and the ongoing interlocking of information systems and sources form that background against which current economic, social and organizational developments (of which specialization is just one) take place. Information is transformed from being a crucial organizational or economic input into an encompassing ecology, a habitat as it were, within which many organizational and economic operations are embedded.

A major implication of the rapidly growing quantity of available information is thus those possibilities it offers for being drawn upon whenever planning or evaluating initiatives and outcomes in particular contexts of contemporary life. Information introduces a 'depth of perspective' consequent upon the possibility of relating and juxtaposing information items and sources. In so doing, however, this increased range of information tends to shift the evaluation of locally-generated courses of action away from the consideration of local or context-embedded factors towards considerations derived from other context-transcending or global concerns increasingly mediated by decontextualized systems of representation (Kallinikos 2004c; Rolland and Monteiro 2002). A specific manifestation of these abstract trends, which I subsumed in Chapter 2 under the notion of disembeddedness, is the global relocating of economic operations and the possibility of running their dispersed and heterogeneous contexts by means of information control rather than traditional hierarchical control or ownership (Beniger 1986; Sassen 2001).

The impregnation of the local, bounded and functionally-simplified character of the core operations of particular settings by information descending from disembedded or decontextualized data sources is an inevitable outcome of such trends. The organizational implications of these developments are, however, more ambiguous. To the degree that such trends lead to the subordination and control of the local and particular to the global and abstract, they produce a substantial set of preconditions for the emergence of centralized systems of control based on information (Brown and Duguid 2000; Sassen 2001; Zuboff 1988). But the availability and accessibility of information may equally render the centre superfluous, to the degree they deprive its coordinative capacity from one of the key functions upon which centralized control is predicated: the gathering, distribution and channelling of information, the latter often in the form of variously processed information codified into decisions, orders or selective messages. The seminal work of Zuboff (1988) still stands as one of the most thorough and elegant studies of these contradictory trends in organizations. The disembedded character of operations, as mediated by technological information, is furthermore complexly related to local practices. The concrete and specific make-up of local practices is often essential in providing an injection of reality which the abstract status of decontextualized forms of representation and interaction often need (Bowker and Star 1999; Suchman 1996).

The double-edged character of the implications of information growth is well illustrated by Knorr-Cetina and Bruegger's (2002)[5] study of foreign currency exchange markets. Their research reveals how the global systems of electronic transactions exemplified by these markets are essentially sustained by what the authors call the social microstructures of traders' lateral interactions. Dialogic, computer-mediated conversations, developing at the interstices of, or beyond, the structural and institutional complexity of the contemporary financial world, are shown to play an essential role in making and executing a variety of decisions associated with the workings of these markets. In so doing, they contribute to overcoming the interpretive ambiguity and other limitations which the decontextualized nature of net-based transactions are prone to engender. Sassen (2001) also provides a captivating account of the decentralizing and recentralizing trends underlying the organization and delivery of financial services in a connected, informatized world. Over the last decades, the management and control of information by major financial players has made a few major metropolitan cities the switchboards of global financial flows and the central nodes of national, regional and global transactions. At the same time, these developments have reasserted the significance of locality. Great metropolitan cities represent dense communicative contexts in which trend dissemination and oral information exchanges of various sorts take place, thus also furnishing an abundance and variety of human talent and skills indispensable to the operations of global finance. The centrality of these cities as financial centres of global reach consequently finds essential support in what has always constituted the essence of the city; its place and resource concentration as distinct from the spatial dispersion of financial transactions.[6]

5. See footnote 16, Chapter 3.
6. It is worth noting that both these studies are about the financial world. We still lack thorough empirical investigations that depict how and to what

More than two decades ago the ambiguous character of the developments put into motion by the process of disembeddedness had already been pointed out by Granovetter (1985). Disembeddedness has a thick tail consisting of the counter tendencies of re-embeddedness that furnish a means of recompensing for those aspects of socioeconomic life (locality, particularity, autonomy) that are suppressed, ignored or excluded, even as disembedded trends push for abstraction, virtuality and centralization (Carrier and Miller 1998). Recall Woolgar's (2002) counter-intuitive claim, mentioned in the preceding chapter, that the more intense the virtual relationships that information and communication technologies promote the greater the need to support their disembedded operations by anchoring them into the tangible and material character of reality (see too Esposito 1996, 2003; Heller 1999; Kallinikos 1996, 1999).

However, it would be a gross simplification to assume that the countervailing power of the two trends eventually cancel out one another. The reassertion of the significance of the local and particular that occurs as the outcome of repairing the breakdowns left behind by disembedded processes, is of an entirely different character from the corresponding processes that occur within what I would refer to, for want of a better term, as primary local contexts. Re-embeddedness is increasingly framed by the overall nexus of conditions which disembedded processes establish (Kallinikos 1996, 2004b). The critical issue then becomes one of understanding and accounting for the new architecture of control that keeps emerging as the result of decontextualized systems and local practices being reassembled into new patterns under the expanding instrumental influence of technological information.

5.4 Disaggregation and Networks

Two broad trends emerge from the comprehensive informatization of organizations and the growth and instrumental significance of technological information depicted above. The first is associated with the immersion of organizational operations in a larger ecology of systems and processes increasingly mediated

extent information is involved in dissolving, decomposing and recomposing the operations of organizations that predominantly produce physical goods (see Kallinikos 1999).

by technological information. The multiple ties thus established have further accentuated the long-standing drift of management away from the centre stage of the production of goods and services. The second trend is clearly expressed by the expanding dissolvability of a large array of tasks and processes, as the outcome of informatization piercing deep into the minute, microscopic texture of organizational operations, decomposing and reconstructing them as a series of computational, automated processes.

Though deriving from seemingly opposing forces which disclose, respectively, an outward versus inward orientation, these two trends reinforce one another. They join hands in questioning, in their own different ways, the making of well-defined instrumental enclosures into the centre of gravity around which organizational operations develop. In so doing, they both expose some of the limitations of the bounded and hierarchically constituted organization as the predominant framework for undertaking, managing and controlling economic operations. On the one hand, the growth of technological information depicted above introduces considerations deriving from a large infospace extending far beyond the confines of core operations. It thus reframes the equilibrium of concerns and relevancies and redefines the strategic position of organizational functions and roles in ways that reflect the significance of external constituencies. On the other hand, the dissolvable character of organizational tasks and processes provides the means for rehearsing the composition of the mix of inputs by which products and services are made, and eventually redistributing them among different and often dispersed organizations. Externally procured services may enjoy significant cost advantages; specialized resources previously beyond reach may become available; and foreign markets might be accessed and penetrated far more smoothly. The resulting mobile and transferable character of a wide range of services and the dynamics of information growth and communication are involved in the steady repositioning of the relative significance which internally produced and externally procured resources or services are acquiring.

Albeit contested and still awaiting persuasive empirical corroboration, disaggregation and vertical disintegration can be seen as organizational manifestations of these changing infrastructural conditions which information as habitat keeps on establishing. In this context, disaggregation could be interpreted as a means for exploring the decomposability of organizational operations, and taking advantage of the possibility of relocating externally a significant number of operations previously conducted in-house. The perception of such opportunities is heavily contingent on the ability granted by interoperable and transferable information to review, inspect and manage a substantially broader spectrum of situations. At the same time the technical infrastructure over which information travels allows for various forms of control and communication over extended functional and geographical zones.

As an organizational strategy, disaggregation could thus be viewed as heavily conditioned by the underlying technological developments that help disband, decouple or relax the tight functional dependencies and the strong geographical embeddedness that have commonly characterized organizational operations. A variety of historically contingent constraints can thus be lifted, establishing the conditions for alternative forms of organizing and pursuing economic objectives (for example, DeSanctis and Monge 1999; Rifkin 2000; Castells 2001). These trends perhaps find the strongest manifestation in the emergence of networks (referred to often as virtual organizations) that subcontract production (and even other operations) in short-lived schemes that can be abandoned as necessary. Virtual organizations exemplify the trend towards permanent disaggregation, in their effort to take advantage of shifting consumer, intermediate or producer markets through the frequent reshuffling and recomposition of the mix of inputs and operations by which products and services are produced (Malone and Laubacher 1998; Mowshowitz 2002). By subcontracting and outsourcing a wide range of production tasks, organizations of this type concentrate on higher order operations such as deciding the type of products to be produced, formulating design characteristics, marketing strategies and the like. Operations of this sort are themselves supported by services procured globally. At the same time, they provide the premises for bringing together the contributions of a variety of spatially dispersed organizations or actors into time-bound and shifting networks that seek to accommodate the sociocultural context of late capitalism on a global scale.

In this sense, virtual organization represents the Other of organizations as bounded, locally-based and hierarchical systems, being characterized instead by dispersion and delocalization, and regulated to a considerable degree by legally-enforceable contracts in the place of a variety of internal rules, regulations and procedures. But it also epitomizes a specific, power-mediated coordinative arrangement in which the initiative of decomposing and recomposing what was once a tightly interwoven set of operations now lies in the hands of those economic agents most able to respond to, or control parts of, the production and distribution of information (Aksoy and Robins 1992; Ekbia and Kling 2005; Rifkin 2000; Zuboff and Maxmin 2003). Even though these developments need not be a zero-sum game, it is reasonable to expect the terms as regards the decomposition–redistribution–recomposition of the mix of inputs of particular products and services to be increasingly set by dominant power holders and corporations. The outsourcing of services and operations does not solely and inevitably reflect the established division of labour within an industry and the gains that accrue by having specialized suppliers delivering what was previously produced in-house.[7] The decision to outsource, as the offshoring of quasi-routine services often demonstrates, may well reflect the relative power in arm's length relationships that ride on, and further accentuate, regional and global differences in the cost and overall conditions of production.

Disaggregation is in this way involved in the establishment of a new architecture of control made possible by the dissolvability, recomposition and redistribution of tasks and operations that were previously conducted within the confines of single organizations. However, as noted, disaggregation rides on a slower, yet long-wave change that is manifested in the deepening separation of non-production functions (such as finance and marketing) from production ones and the rising importance of the former at the expense of the latter (Fligstein 1990). Such a separation, I have suggested, obtains new dimensions due to the instrumental significance of information that increasingly immerses organizational operations within a greater ecology of relations and processes. Under these conditions, the once vital operations of producing goods and services tend to lose their historic significance and become subordinated to a much wider and evasive logic that is involved in moving the centre of organizational operations away from the instrumental enclosures of production (Baudrillard 1988; Carrier and Miller 1998).[8]

7. That is, what the economies treat under the notion of externalities.
8. The degree to which externalities versus power is the major force that

Power practices of this sort are of course not unknown to powerful industrial complexes (Perrow 1986, 2002). But certain crucial differences seem to be involved. Power in industrial complexes was usually associated with the centrality of the production unit to which, to a large degree, suppliers and distributors were tied, as in the automobile industry. By contrast, what confers on the sort of networks described above the distinctive capacity as hubs is their evasiveness rather than their centrality. Or, perhaps more correctly, their centrality is of an entirely different character, one predicated upon the mastery of the information and communication flows and the ability to provide, in one way or another, the strategic context (that is, the operational premises) for other organizations. Such an ability is closely related to the dissociation of such networks from production facilities. Now the effects of these developments are, as already suggested, complex and ambiguous. Much remains contingent on a number of specific and local features that reflect the processes by which the range of operations making up the network become re-embedded in a variety of local contexts. These variations notwithstanding, the general trend these developments epitomize seems to be towards a new architecture of control, underlain by the ascent of technological information to become a major means for structuring and monitoring dispersed and diversified operations. Under these conditions, throughput operations will tend to be dissociated from all those processes and transactions that develop within the growing domain of information and communication and be subordinated to them.

Developments of this sort are not limited to the corporate world. The organizational trends which disaggregation epitomizes seem to have impinged upon the role of the state and the organization and delivery of public services (Barry 2001; Castells 2001).[9] The idea that the contemporary state can exercise political

drives economic developments represents an intricate issue within a highly contested terrain. For further details see Perrow (2002) and the controversy of Storper (1989, 1993) with Aksoy and Robins (1992).

9. To be sure the rethinking of the role of the state combines with even wider processes impacting upon the sovereignty of the nation state in an increasingly globalized world. The information and communication processes I have analysed in this volume are obviously associated with globalization. Also some of these trends are associated with the wider acceptance of neoliberal ideas and the diffusion of new public management. For obvious reasons, I cannot enter that debate here.

leadership through the control of decision premises and the shaping of communication and information flows rather than through immediate economic and administrative involvement has, over the last quarter-century, won acceptance beyond the neoliberal advocates of the minimal state (see for example, Barry 2001; Fountain 2001). In a sense, the disaggregation and contracting-out of public services preceded the recent upsurge of technological information. They have however been variously related to the modularization of a wide range of services, and they have been given a new momentum by the diffusion of inter-operable information infrastructures, the internet and the organizational transformations these have instigated.

Placed against such a backdrop, this disaggregation of public organizations and state agencies that has taken place over the last two or three decades may acquire a slightly different meaning. The straightforward privatization of public entities or the creation of cross-organizational architectures known as quasi-markets (LeGrand and Bartlett 1993; Osborne and Gaebler 1992) may be seen as a manifestation of the changing architecture of control enabled by the growth of technological information and its organizational implications. In such a model, state functions and the agencies that embody them can be conceived predominantly as coordination centres, whose major task is to provide the necessary premises for other actors' actions and decisions, through the shape of information flows, the making and transmission of higher order decisions and the monitoring of their implementation. The power and coordinating capacity of these centres has been assumed to derive not from immediate involvement with, and steering of, core and often locally-embedded processes and decisions but from the control of the very premises on which the latter are predicated. To accomplish this task, coordination centres should therefore remain both dissociated and detached from local engagements. They should seek to obtain a bird's-eye view of the actors and operations which they coordinate, a task that is substantially aided by the control and management of information processes.[10]

10. Such a task is far more complex and insidious than it may first appear. The subcontracting of a variety of services that were previously provided by public firms and organizations to private firms has necessitated the construction of a complex edifice of specifications with respect to the quality, price and delivery terms of these services and an elaborate system of procedures for monitoring compliance with these specifications (see for

There are certainly important elements of normative pressure, and often a strong ideological predilection, behind the reformation of the public sector along these predominantly new public management lines (Du Gay 2005). Yet the specific direction along which the entrenched interests drive these developments transcends the effects of sheer ideology, and cannot exclusively be accounted for in such terms without postulating fundamental changes in the workings of late capitalism. Some of these changes are ultimately associated with the significance which information continually obtains in the contemporary world. The increasing pliability and decomposability of the economic and organizational operations that it helps bring about establishes a substantially different task infrastructure which, in combination with the communicative facilities current technology provides, promote a new architecture of control.

A close examination of the *modus operandi* of virtual organizations and the broad spectrum of changes associated with the instrumental significance of information suggests a few further observations. The variety of electronically supported arrangements that are involved in the provision of consumer services (e-auctions, virtual stores, portals and the like) indicates that the developments I have sought to summarize above impinge upon the functioning of the market as well (for example, Malone and Laubacher 1998; Rifkin 2000; Sassen 2001). In cases involving the provision of specialized services (recurrent or episodic) between or among organizations, electronic exchanges of this sort are, indeed, difficult to distinguish from the formation of networks. Given the central place of firms in the market economy, it would be reasonable to expect that the changes mentioned in the mode of operations of firms and other organizations would have been reflected in the processes and regulative mechanisms of market exchange (Ciborra 1993). But the forms through which some of the developments depicted above are implicated in the functioning of the market seem to signal a new, hybrid logic that departs significantly from the way markets are posited to operate in theory, if not in practice.

example Clarke 2005; Clarke and Newman 1997; Newman 2005). Many of these procedures are triggered by the normative character of the public sector (for example, health services) whose multi-ethical status comprises a quite different system from that of the market (see for example Chapman 2000; Du Gay 2005; Kallinikos 2006b).

According to Rifkin (2000), a significant segment of electroni-
cally-mediated commercial transactions promotes a distinctive
mode of economic exchange that is predicated on the logic of
access (leased use of services or products) as distinct from the
free exchange of goods and services characteristic of traditional
markets. Access is an activity that runs on time, presupposes
repeated use and does not entail the exchange of ownership
which buying implies. From this view, access-based transactions
are particularly germane to the formation of centralized
networks as they tend to establish long-term relationships,
whereupon users (not buyers) pay a rent (not buy) for accessing
resources or knowledge commanded by specific corporations.
Agriculture (seed reproduction), medicine (biotechnology),
database management, publishing and business format franchis-
ing are typical examples of fields that are particularly suscepti-
ble to networking, built upon Rifkin's (2000) logic of access.

Networks of this sort take on the form of a spider's web,
where a significant number of peripheral units are tied to a
central node. Thus understood, networks emerge as centralized
forms of governance mediated by contemporary information
and communication infrastructures rather than decentralized,
distributed patterns of interaction. If, according to the view
advanced earlier in this chapter, the network calls into question
the administrative legacy of the bounded and hierarchical organization, in Rifkin's (2000) account, centrally-regulated access to
a focal unit challenges the logic of the market as a decentralized,
locally-sensitive system of spot exchanges (Hayek 1945). Rifkin's
(2000) account is, I suggest, indicative of the wider implications
of the economic and social involvement of information and
communication technologies that transcend the confines of organizations, impinging upon other central modes of governance
and institutions in the contemporary world. Seen in this light,
networks are as much an alternative to organizations as they are
to markets.

5.5   Further Remarks on Disaggregation and Networks

In the preceding pages I have assumed that there is a relatively
straightforward connection between the technological developments that are manifested through the growing significance of
technological information, on the one hand, and the disaggregation of organizations and the diffusion of networks as novel

organizational arrangements, on the other. Such a connection I have claimed is mediated by the changing task infrastructure that informatization brings about and the new architectures of communication and control that can be built upon it. However, the ideological struggles that have accompanied the disaggregation (and privatization) of a variety of activity domains previously controlled by the state cast doubts as to whether the power game I described above with reference to the private sector is as univocal and technologically driven as I may have implied.

In the next two chapters I examine in some detail the overall institutional context within which disaggregation and networks develop. Before I embark on this task however, it is important to point out that the dissolvability and mobility of organizational operations consequent upon informatization, to which I attribute such a central significance, is neither an entirely recent nor an isolated phenomenon. The relevant developments take place against the background of a deep division of labour that has furnished important preconditions for the further segmentation and codification of many tasks and operations that coincide with informatization. While giving the prevailing division of labour a new and decisive turn, informatization would never have been possible without the deep and continuing segmentation of tasks and operations produced over the course of industrial capitalism. Furthermore, as I have already indicated, disaggregation, as an organizational strategy, has antecedents in the much more specific and historically contingent developments that have been manifested in the elaborate functional and structural differentiation of organizations. Over the course of industrial capitalism, such a dissociation has been given a solid status by the institutionalization of management functions as a distinct domain of a highly valuable ensemble of operations, indispensable to organizational goal achievement. The ongoing separation of the management of information and communication processes from the core operations of an organization rides on the historical development of the progressive functional and structural dissociation of these two major domains (Chandler 1962, 1977; Mintzberg 1979; Thompson 1967).[11]

11. The functional and structural differentiation of organizations as manifested in the separation of production from non-production functions is intimately related to the construction of instrumental enclosures that I analysed in Chapter 2 in terms of functional simplification and closure.

Therefore, functional and structural differentiation of organizations constitutes the structural antecedent of the current developments, whereby vital information and communication processes take place at an increasing distance from the core processes by which goods and services are produced. The functional and structural differentiation of these two blocks of operations is a prerequisite for further dissociating them and even completely separating them (either administratively or in terms of ownership) to achieve the promise of substantial financial gains or other kinds of benefits. The relative importance which management functions have achieved over the course of industrial capitalism suggests, perhaps, that the terms under which disaggregation takes place are bound to be shaped considerably by management's long-term experience in controlling and shaping information processes.

The character of current developments acquires substantially novel qualities as technological information penetrates deeper and deeper into the fabric of the prevailing economic, organizational and institutional relations. In this sense, information is much more than just an important input or resource. It provides a new technologically-mediated mode of perceiving and acting upon the world, whose significance permeates a wide range of institutions, operations and activity systems. As I have claimed throughout this chapter, information increasingly becomes a habitat. However, the pressures which the technological developments associated with the rising significance of information exercise upon the prevailing organizational arrangements and upon the institutions supporting them make necessary a closer examination of the institutional and organizational order of modernity. The next two chapters deal with these issues.

Recall that these two principles are crucially involved in the separation of the technical from the social system in organizations. This in turn constitutes a prerequisite for further dissociating production from non-production functions.

6. Addendum on Networks and Institutions

6.1 Formal Organizations as Modern Institutions

The observations advanced in the preceding chapter suggest that the diffusion of networks as organizational arrangements reflects a variety of developments that are closely associated with the possibilities information offers for reframing and reorganizing the production of goods and services in the contemporary world. However, economic and organizational change of this scale does not occur in a vacuum. I have noted several times throughout this volume that the implications of the continuing information growth dynamics are conditioned by the predominant cultural and institutional relationships which are the outcome of long-standing social and economic developments. It is therefore necessary to look a bit more closely at how the prevailing institutions accommodate the challenges which current technological developments raise.

I take an institution to represent the solidification of ideas, informal behaviour patterns or practices into time-persisting social arrangements that, thus solidified, provide the regulative and normative framework for subsequent social conduct (for example, marriage, money, voting, the employment contract). The establishment of an institution thus implies the extraction of a particular aspect of social life from the hazy and informal background of social significations, relations or practices and the attribution to it of a specific status (Searle 1995) so as to render it solid, recognizable and, crucially, authoritative. The attribution of such a status or specific function to an aspect of social life is not simply an act of will. Rather, it represents a complex and value-laden social process that involves the assignment of priorities and the development of legal and administrative mechanisms essential for governing social conduct according to the principles, standards and regulations an institution embodies

(Hasselbladh and Kallinikos 2000). I cannot here hope to deal with the vexed issues which institutions and the various institutional theories raise (see for example Castoriadis 1987; Douglas 1986; Hasselbladh and Kallinikos 2000; Powell and DiMaggio 1991; Scott 1995). It is nevertheless necessary to state, as clearly as possible, my view of institutions and bring it to bear on the issues of how network arrangements fit within the wider institutional picture of late modernity and capitalism which they are supposed to challenge.

An important implication that follows from my view of institutions is the clear distinction between institutions as, on the one hand, a set of habits, routines and typifications, and on the other hand, formal social arrangements supported by legal, administrative and other procedural mechanisms.[1] Habits, routines and typifications do represent the objectification of action patterns into behavioural moulds that provide stability and recurrence in social life. In this sense, habituation, routine making and typification could be seen as instances of institutionalization. However, neither of these would, of themselves, imply the development of elaborate legal and administrative mechanisms to support them, even though routines in the context of social and organizational life may occasionally do so. Habits, routines and typifications represent the crystallization of an inter-subjective, power-mediated order that embodies the lessons of experience. Such a view of institutions stems clearly from the interactionist legacy that Berger and Luckmann (1966) have left, and represents undeniably a valuable approach for studying the social construction of micro-orders. But it is less well attuned to capturing wider institutional processes that entail the imbrications of structural, political and economic processes evolving in large time spans.

Therefore, the view of institutions I embrace is not one concerned with the construction of the micro-order of organizations. It is rather one that considers as preconditions crucial to institution building: firstly, the legal and regulative forms by which a status is assigned to a specific aspect of social life; and secondly the administrative and procedural mechanisms by which such a status is monitored and enforced. Institutions are uniformities that must be brought into being and governed. Placed in such a context, networks confront a landscape

1. I am indebted to Hans Hasselbladh for raising my awareness on this issue.

predominantly made of the institutional arrangement of the formal organization and the legal and administrative patterns or forms through which formal organizations are constituted and rendered as accountable social entities.[2] Accountability is supported by a variety of legal and administrative procedures, yet one institutional process seems to be a crucial prerequisite: the granting of a well-defined jurisdictional responsibility on the basis of which a social entity can be rendered accountable. In the context of formal organizations, indeed in the context of modern life in general, jurisdictional responsibility is closely tied to the institution of property rights, though the legislative assignment of jurisdiction and the enforcement of property rights are complexly intertwined with political, social and administrative processes too (Fligstein 2001; Lessig 2002; North 1990).

The formal status of organizations in modernity must therefore be seen as integral to the project of constructing the social uniformities necessary to support the administrative and legal accountability of a considerable range of social entities (Du Gay 2005; Gellner 1996; Jepperson and Meyer 1991). This admittedly brief description of the social order of formal organizations would, however, remain flawed without the consideration of the central character which the labour or employment contract has assumed in organizational governance. The employment contract provides the terms by which individuals are involved in organizations as employees and delineates the rights and obligations they have vis-à-vis the organization. There is little doubt that the employment contract represents the outcome of a long-standing struggle on the part of employees (through trade unions) to negotiate the terms of their involvement in organizations. But as an institution, the employment contract has been rendered possible by the overall framework of accountability which the legal-rational regulative regime of formal organization has been able to support. As I suggest in some detail in the next chapter, accountability and the legal-rational regime it presupposes are essential aspects of governing social relationships in modernity.

2. Jepperson (1991) raises some concerns as to whether formal organization could be considered as an institution. His view of formal organization, I gather, is narrower than the one I advance here and it seems to me largely to coincide with what I call an organizational arrangement. I return to these issues in the next chapter, where I deal with bureaucracy as an essential aspect of the formal character of modern organizations.

The severe demands imposed by the accomplishment of short-term organizational objectives often force into the background the institutional embeddedness of organizations. Organizational activities are, as a rule, immersed in the muddy character of a variety of exigencies driven by the quest for efficiency that permeates everyday practice. From this point of view, the prevailing structural arrangements and modes of work in organizations seem to derive overwhelmingly from the harsh reality of underlying functional and economic circumstances and the target and performance demands these inflict. Organizations tend to be seen as no more than functional–structural assemblages, whose morphology is the outcome of a consequential logic of adaptation to the prevailing conditions. Placed against such a backdrop, the institutional status of organizations becomes too abstract or evasive and slips easily beyond observation and consideration.

Generally, the impact of technological information on organizations has been understood in such predominantly functional–structural terms, as the literature reviewed in the preceding chapter suggests. The diffusion of information, along with the technologies by which it is supported, is assumed to exert strong pressures upon the functional–structural arrangements of organizations (compartmentalization, vertical division of labour, job and role differentiation, boundary maintenance) to accommodate the possibilities created by technological change. But what can we say about the character of these organizations as formal, institutional entities? Do these trends really imply the historical decline and marginalization and perhaps the eventual extinction of the formal status of the unitary, bounded and hierarchical character of organizations? Do institutions like formal organizations change in a substantial fashion as the cumulative outcome of structural changes? Or how do the structural and institutional realms bear upon one another?

6.2 Functions, Structures, Institutions

To respond to the above questions, I find it relevant to venture a distinction between two widely divergent approaches to social and economic reality that are broadly recognized within social theory. However, the indiscriminate conflation of the substantially different understanding of current developments which these approaches imply has tended to produce a certain confusion with respect to the prospects facing formal organizations. The same holds true as regards the interpretation of networks and the role the latter are assumed to play in the process of restructuring the organizational order of modernity.

The first of these approaches, deriving mainly from economics and functionalist sociology, sees the development of new organizational forms as arrangements that seek to minimize the cost of social interaction through a process of negotiations, ultimately rooted in the rational consideration of the world (Arrow 1974). In this view, formal organizations (and networks) are understood as less or more effective organizational arrangements whose prospects are closely tied to the possibilities they offer for addressing efficiently the production of goods and services. Over longer time spans, less efficient arrangements are assumed to give way gradually to more efficient ones, as the basic ordering principle of rationality, ultimately supported by the market, structures the preoccupations and the choices of social agents (see for example Arrow 1974; Castells 2001; Fukuyama 1997). Under these conditions, the remaking of organizational arrangements is assumed to take place largely in an institutional context that is significantly malleable. The institutional impediments such a remaking confronts are in principle negotiable. Institutions, if they exist at all, are no more than provisional agreements between rational actors, and are therefore open to renegotiation in the light of any rationally justified evidence that demands their revision (North 1981, 1990; Williamson 1985).

The second approach sees formal organizations as impregnated by institutions in ways that produce a less tractable social reality. Institutions are more than just rationally arrived agreements, freely open to negotiation and reconstruction. In solidifying reality, institutions embody values and ideologies and are provisional settlements only in a historical sense. The cultural, ethical and cognitive orientations that institutions embody interlock with legal and administrative mechanisms and powerful economic interests to make them hardly negotiable in the short term. According to this view, the organizational arrangements associated with formal organizations are the outcome of social compromises reached over longer time spans, often involving considerable social lock-ins and scarcely reversible path dependencies. Social compromises may well be motivated by, and entail the pursuit of, benefit and goal maximization, yet only as

these last are understood within the dominant cultural para-
digm(s) and the institutions so produced. Viewed from this institutional perspective, formal organizations are not just
functional–structural assemblages entailing relationships
between functions, task modules and roles. Rather, they are
instantiations of institutional arrangements. Their operations are
accordingly underlain by a complex and historically cumulated
system of rules, laws and regulations governing the relationships of organizational participants as members of democratic
societies (see for example Du Gay 2005; Fligstein 2001; Jepperson
and Meyer 1991; Meyer 1994).

The adoption of this second position does not rule out the
impact which functional and structural forces may have upon an
established social and institutional order. Social life does change
and under conditions in which functional and structural considerations gather momentum, they can come to exercise significant
pressure for institutional change. The technological and organizational developments I have considered in the preceding chapters exemplify this process of technological, organizational and
institutional friction. In the literature concerning networks, there
has been a tendency, however, to underplay the significance
played by institutions and simplify the burdensome character of
institutional change (for example, Castells 1996, 2000; Fukuyama
1997).

The unitary, bounded and hierarchically constituted organization which networks are assumed to challenge can be seen as a
particular instance of formal organization: a historically contingent embodiment of this institutional arrangement.[3] As an
instance of an institution, the unitary, bounded and hierarchically constituted organization cannot be modified in any
substantial fashion solely in terms of an adaptivist logic, reflecting rational calculations of what is functionally more efficient.
As made clear in the preceding section, formal organizations
operate under a legal–rational regime that stipulates the duties
and rights of organizational participants (employers and
employees) and provides a variety of rules, laws and regulations

---

3. I consider the bounded and hierarchical organization as historically contin-
    gent in the sense that governance through formal means could have
    assumed forms other than bounded and hierarchical. In other words, there
    is no intrinsic relationship between formality, on the one hand, and bound-
    edness and hierarchy, on the other. For more details, see the next chapter.

by means of which organizational operations are governed. Most crucially, organizations emerge as institutional entities (as opposed to sheer functional–structural arrangements) on the basis of the jurisdictional–legal responsibility they embody, thanks to which they are rendered accountable, both in an administrative and a legal sense (Du Gay 2005; Fountain 2001; Perrow 1986). Therefore any substantial modification of formal organization would render necessary the considerable renegotiation of this intricate and solidified order that maintains, in addition, a variety of bonds with other institutions across the institutional landscape of modern society.

6.3 A Note on Bureaucracy versus Networks

Formal organizations are, to introduce another terminology, bureaucracies, and their status as formal social entities is essentially sustained by their bureaucratic constitution (Weber 1947, 1978). The dominant understanding of bureaucracy is unfortunately highly stylized and considerably simplified. It tends to view bureaucracy as a largely introvert and ossified social form. Such a view has led to the belief that the rule-based and legal regulation of bureaucracies (the corporation is a form of bureaucracy) are either a vice or just a remnant of the past. Accordingly, a widespread assumption is that the bureaucratically constituted organization may not possess adequate flexibility to respond to the demands for shifting and scalable forms of engagement which the developments outlined in the preceding chapter make increasingly necessary. Strict adherence to rules, hierarchical command and centralized decision making do not resonate well with the demands raised by current technological and economic developments. The outcome of this friction is supposed to be leading to a new institutional order expressed in deregulation, the liberalization of labour law, flexible forms of employment and less strict accountability regimes. Taken collectively, these institutional developments are presumed to be driven by the new economic and technological realities and the functional prerequisites underlying the operations of networks, as these last are manifested in the steadily shifting decomposition and recomposition of the resources that make up the output of the network. Widespread as it is, such an account nevertheless derives from a predominantly economic and functionalist understanding of institutions and unduly simplifies the agonistic, cumbersome and ambiguous nature of institutional change. It is, in addition, predicated on a largely inadequate understanding of bureaucracy and formal organization.

Though I devote the next chapter exclusively to bureaucracy, which I consider to be the dominant organizational form in modernity, it is necessary to provide here a shorthand view of this central modern institution, as a means of gaining a better appreciation of the issues raised by disaggregation and the diffusion of networks. The tight regulative regime governing formal organizations often tends to conceal the functional efficacy and technical superiority of the bureaucratic form (Reed 2005). Intimately tied to the dynamic character of modernity, the bureaucratic constitution of formal organizations represents a historically unique form of governing social relations. It is the only organizational form known to humanity that has systematically separated the requirements of organizational role incumbents from the person, conceived as an existential or anthropological unity (Gellner 1996; Kallinikos 2003, 2004a). As I claim in considerable detail in the next chapter, the bureaucratic constitution of formal organizations has been historically contingent upon the non-inclusive involvement of individuals in organizations. Such a mode of involvement both expresses and embodies the differentiation of work from other civic engagements. At the same time, it is implicated in the regulation of organizational membership in rational–legal terms that are broadly concordant with the liberal spirit of modern democratic societies. From this perspective, the administrative machinery of earlier times cannot qualify as bureaucracies in the Weberian sense. There are no medieval, Chinese or Egyptian bureaucracies, despite this being often awkwardly claimed, at least not in the sense in which Weber (1947, 1978) intended the term. Ancient or older administrative systems may have been quite complex and potent administrative machineries, but not bureaucracies as legal–rational regimes, in which the organizational role and its exercise are systematically separated from the person conceived as an anthropological unity (Luhmann 1995).

Through the separation of the role from the person, bureaucracy has enabled a sufficient dissociation of the re-engineering of tasks and roles from the time-consuming and socially and psychologically cumbersome processes of personal reorientation. In so doing, it has provided the space for the ceaseless remaking of organizational arrangements without immediate social or personal impediments. The flexibility of bureaucracy, as historically witnessed by the dynamic and constantly unfolding character of the modern social order, is unmatched by all other forms of organization in which human involvement takes inclusive forms.[4] On the other hand, the heavily regulated practices of role re-engineering and the demands of accountability underlying the legal–rational regime that governs the operations of the bureaucratic form may feel severely constraining. In any case, excessive regulation does not seem to be well attuned to the demands for the mobile, decomposable and scalable arrangements that are being diffused, as the outcome of the developments outlined in the preceding chapter.

How do networks fit into this complex picture? Are the technological, functional and economic realities which networks epitomize going to demand the thorough renegotiation of the prevailing organizational order of modernity and the institutions sustaining it? As the preceding section makes clear, there is no straightforward answer to the issue concerning the conflict between the re-engineering of social reality that functionality drives and its preservation by the established institutional order. Yet, a few considerations could be advanced. Placed against the background of the definition of the formal organization given above, the organizational arrangement of the network scarcely qualifies as an organizational form. Even though network relationships may be formalized in a variety of contracts, the network lacks jurisdictional responsibility which would lend it a formal status. For as far as profit appropriation is associated with the corporate form (Kraakman 2001), and work is predominantly carried out in institutional settings regulated by employment contracts (no matter how flexible or time limited) it is difficult to think of networks as an alternative to formal organization. Unless the network is constituted as a unit of jurisdictional responsibility (which would require its transformation into some sort of formal organization) it is destined to remain no more than a social arrangement or practice; a strategy, as it were, for the reallocation of resources in a highly volatile economy

---

4. That is, total organizations, elements of which have reappeared in the form of a culture of overwork in which job concerns strongly dominate and in some cases exclude other personal interests or preoccupations (Beck 2000; Carnoy 2000; Kallinikos 2003; Kunda 1992). I elaborate on this issue in the next chapter.

within which information and communication processes assume primary importance.

These considerations suggest that networks may not represent an alternative organizational form but rather the necessary organizational strategy for exploring the possibilities of organizing operations in shifting and recombinable forms. Goods and services are destined to continue to be produced within organizations as institutional entities (that is, corporations, public organizations, authorities and so on), even though the structural templates of these entities may come to change as the outcome of the developments that are analysed in this volume. Indeed, the crucial effects networks may bring are not to be sought in the alternative form of organization which they are assumed to provide instead of bureaucracy, if by form is meant an institutionally embedded organization with jurisdictional responsibility and a well-developed societal framework of laws, rules and regulations decreeing its operations. If the concept of form is, on the other hand, used in the general sense of an arrangement, then the network as a temporary, project-based alliance of actors could well be understood as a form. However, in this case, the network would be more of an alternative to the market than to the bureaucracy. Networks, in that respect, have always existed (see for example Garnham 1990, 2004; Tilly 2001), even though currently a case could be made for the rising importance which information and communication processes assume and the shifting or scalable, network-like forms of management and collaboration that such processes render necessary.

Social and institutional change is, as a rule, a painful process for the simple reason that it involves the redistribution of entrenched rights and obligations that may affect the life prospects and chances of many. Any change towards the direction of making formal organizations less salient institutions than they have been over the last century may demand the renegotiation of a significant part of the established institutional order (for example, labour law, employment contracts, pension schemes, forms of accountability and democratic representation and others). Little wonder, some of these changes have already crept into the scene; others may look more complex and remote. Contemplating the current developments and the prospect of the decline of formal organizations and the state as key modern institutions ensuring civic rights, accountability in public life and equality, Tilly (2001: 210) concludes that the 'implications for democracy are chilling . . . when it comes to anticipating twenty first century qualities and textures of life, the stakes are high' (see also Beck 1992; Kallinikos 2003; Sennett 2006).

6.4 Formal Organizations, Modernity and Beyond

How, then, can we gauge the relationship between the dynamics of information growth analysed in this volume and its organizational implications? The consequences of these developments may not be exhausted in those changes that are associated with the decomposability, exchangeability and combinability of organizational operations and the disaggregation of organizations. As the admittedly sketchy observations put forth in the preceding sections suggest, the diffusion of networks as an alternative organizational arrangement that underpins these developments is immersed in a thick institutional order by which it is accommodated in a variety of ways.

The relationship between an institutional order and the organizational arrangements it is associated with is but a specific manifestation of a wider sociological problem: how institutions frame and accommodate or alternatively are accommodated, challenged and perhaps transcended by the material, functional and structural exigencies by which they are underlain. The two basic positions I sketched earlier in this chapter represent responses to this fundamental question. The first privileges the nexus of material, functional and economic conditions and the dynamics they give rise to as the major force of social engineering. The second grants institutions the dominant role in the reproduction of the social order.[5] However, the relationship between the two is much more insidious than it may seem in the first instance. For what is perceived and understood as material or functional may itself be the outcome of cultural predispositions expressed by and rooted in an institutional order. Indeed, functionality could itself be seen as a major institution, in the sense of construing and projecting a particular understanding of

---

5. This problem has philosophical ramifications and it is implicated in the relationship between the material conditions of life and the wider social and institutional relationships within which the inescapable materiality of life is accommodated. Marx once gauged this relationship in the now widely-known terms of base and superstructure. He recognized both yet finally privileged the role of the base, which he referred to as the forces of production.

life, rooted in a particular system of values and supported by a range of legal forms and administrative and organizational arrangements (Castoriadis 1987).

In short, the problem raised by the diffusion of networks represents but a specific manifestation of a much wider and long-lasting problematic. Even the two major positions that have been developed in the literature as regards the relationship of technology to society (technological determinism versus social reductionism) carry the heavy repercussions of this fundamental controversy. I have in the preceding chapter and others sought to navigate between these two extreme, perhaps ideal, positions. There is little doubt that the current developments epitomized by the rising instrumental significance of technological informa-tion take place within a complex institutional matrix. However, such a matrix accommodates and constrains but does not nullify the importance of technological information. It is reasonable to conjecture that as the developments epitomized by the growth of organizations and their deep penetration by technological infor-mation gain momentum they will come to exercise strong pres-sure upon the prevailing institutional relations for change. While variously accommodated by the institutional order within which it develops, technology matters. Seen particularly from a long-term perspective, the overall dynamics that technology sets into motion are not amenable to full control and are only modestly accountable in terms of the social strategies and the interests of social groups alone.

It would indeed be tempting to think that disaggregation and the institutional implications associated with the remaking, or even decline, of formal organization as a key institution of the modern social order could be just the beginning of a long-wave change encompassing far-reaching social and institutional trans-formations. The orientation of modern life that coincides with the rising significance of technological information reflects long-standing developments that reorganize the human sensorium and the social apparatus by which the world is perceived and acted upon (Cooper 1989; Flusser 2000, 2003). If the self-propelling dynamics of information growth that have been taking place over the last decades continue unabated, and it is hard to believe that they will not, then information will come to redefine the entire micro-texture of contemporary life, giving rise to a new realm of human intervention in the world. Placed in such a context, information ordering and reduction ought to become increasingly vital and economically rewarding tasks, irrespective of any utility they may have for the production and distribution of goods and services. Information ordering and information services will thus become valuable and constantly expanding operations in their own right and tied straightforwardly to consumption without having to be redeemed by production (Baudrillard 1988; Virilio 2000). One might even go further and suggest that the growing significance of technologically-mediated forms of interaction might well lead to the increasing infiltration of the principle of economic performance by a significantly less consequential logic that reflects the development of communicative, information-based transactions and the consumption of images as a largely autonomous, self-propelling domain. Here the information age joins hands with postmodernity, as the boundaries of what were once different domains of economy, culture and society become increasingly blurred (Baudrillard 1988; Bauman 1992; Virilio 2000).

Let us, however, return to the key questions that concern us here. As construed in this volume, networks and networking practices reflect the confluence of several economic, social and technological developments. The claim, though, that suggests that networks are 'the operating system of the information economy' (Castells 2002: xxx) is not easy to support. The network is not, as yet, an institutional fold in the same way that markets and bureaucracies, the state or professions[6] have been. Current economic and organizational life presupposes the continuance of all those legal forms and institutions that have sustained economic operations prior to the information age. Property rights, labour contracts, other legal contracts, hierarchy albeit perhaps flattened, jurisdictional distributions, systems of accountability and reporting are all going to persist, modified to a greater or lesser degree, as the building blocks of organizations in the economy and society of the information age. Rather than representing the 'cells of economic activity', in the fashion of firms and formal organizations, networks could be seen as arrangements reflecting the quest for cross-boundary transac-

6. I have deliberately refrained from analysing the role of professions as a means of keeping the complexity of the volume at reasonable levels. The contribution of professions in the construction of the modern organizational order has been so central that it necessitates its own treatment. See for example, Abbott (1988) and Freidson (2001).

tions involving mostly the exchange, transfer and generation of messages and information. Such a quest is, itself, motivated by the dissociation of key management functions from the exigencies of the throughput operations consequent upon the comprehensive computational rendition of reality and the spectacular growth of information such a rendition gives rise to. These developments signal a different division of labour and new architectures of control whose growing momentum will increasingly be reflected by the market economy, the organization of the state and the management of public agencies.[7]

How precisely these changes will come to be manifested, it seems premature to state. The fuller understanding of the issues that have been raised so far makes necessary the far more lengthy and detailed consideration of the bureaucratic organization and the many and intricate ties it maintains with modernity and its institutional order. I turn to this task in the next chapter.

7. See Chapters 3 and 4.

7.   The Organizational Order of Modernity[1]

7.1   Setting the Stage

Bureaucracy is a central institution of the modern world that represents a distinctive and historically specific form of governing social relations. Bureaucracy governs through a variety of institutionally-anchored mechanisms that crucially recount the formal character of modern life. By formal, I here refer to those impersonal, sufficiently standardized and accountable transactions between members of society that act under specific presuppositions, including as employees, professionals, clients or delegates. In this sense, I deploy the term *bureaucracy* as largely synonymous with formal organization to refer to social entities (most notably firms and public agencies) that operate under a specific regime of rules and regulations, as the outcome of the jurisdictional responsibility granted to them through legal, administrative or political processes (Blau 1955, 1957; Fountain 2001; Weber 1947, 1978). Other major forms of regulating the formal character of social relations in the modern world are the institutions of the law and the market. Obviously, formal organizations, markets and the law are interrelated, and, in a variety of ways, they bear upon one another. Most crucially, perhaps, all three are predicated upon a general societal education, capable of granting a majority of the population a high level of standardized cognitive or technical skills and, in this process, cultivating those predispositions essential to sustain the operations of these institutions (Gellner 1983).

As a means of regulating social relations, formality should neither be equated to indifference nor be understood as

1. Some core ideas of this chapter were first published in the journal *Organization* with the title *The Social Foundations of the Bureaucratic Order* (Kallinikos 2004a). The present chapter draws on this article but deviates from it in some important respects.

empty-handed, ceremonial behaviour that is devoid of meaning. Formality certainly entails a mode of relating that stands at the other end from intimacy and social relations that are governed by loyalty, passion or emotions (Hirschman 1977). Given the strong negative inheritance which romanticism has left on our understanding of formal relations, it is worth stressing that formality is a fundamental mode of relating to others in a society like ours, in which a large part of one's everyday encounters are with strangers or non-intimates – people outside one's own limited circle of friends and relatives. It is important not to lose sight of the fundamental fact that the advent of the modern social order coincided with the transition from the world of segmented societies, organized in locally-based communities of fixed roles and positions, to the open and socially mobile character of large social aggregates and the formation of the nation state (Gellner 1983; Giddens 1990; Luhmann 1982).[2] The impersonal social space of modernity is the outcome of the breaking with tradition which such a transition, by necessity, implied. Formality, in this impersonal space, is civility. It is the recognition that the more-or-less transient transactions that constitute the fabric of modern life should be conducted and concluded in as smooth and frictionless a fashion as possible.

Seen in this light, bureaucracy has represented a key means to embody formality and govern social relationships in the modern world. As an institution, bureaucracy has been integral to modernity, providing the platform for constructing the social uniformities that ensure the legal and administrative accountability of formal organizations and the predictability of their operations. Bureaucracy has in addition been variously implicated in the constitution of modern citizens as free and accountable subjects (Du Gay 2000, 2005), a condition that many people easily overlook or even find hard to understand. Freedoms and rights are modern (and for that reason inevitably Western) inventions, contrived uniformities, as Du Gay (2005: 7) describes them, being constructed, consolidated and enforced through a variety of formal mechanisms, among which bureaucracy is a

---

2. I simplify here the painful, agonizing and in some ways variable nature of this transition. Yet, in these broad brush strokes, this picture captures key elements of the transition to modernity and is essential for comprehending the social ground upon which formality and bureaucracy are founded. For more details see Gellner (1983, 1996) and Giddens (1990).

central one. It is not by accident that in his account of bureaucracy, Weber (1947, 1978) describes, in essence, key aspects of the
modern society. Whether in state administration or the consolidated capitalist enterprise, the bureaucratic form of organization
represents a crucial means for structuring and regulating social
relationships in modernity.

The negative undertones that permeate the common assessment of bureaucracy represent a complex and, in a sense, strange
alliance of historically sedimented reactions against formality
that cut across a wide spectrum of domains and political ideologies in modernity (Kallinikos 2004a; Sennett 2006). Critical
humanism and artistic aversion to bureaucratic systems have
joined hands with left-inspired criticism of the organizational
practices of capitalism and statism to construct an image of
bureaucracy as an institution inimical to human dignity.
According to such a view, bureaucracy is both labyrinthine in its
operational complexity and unresponsive to the needs of
humanity. Being the extended arm of power, it is an institution
of oppression that stifles freedom and perpetuates social
inequalities (Adorno and Horkheimer 1972/1937; Castoriadis
1985, 1987; Marcuse 1955). For clearly different, though not unrelated reasons, bureaucracy has been viewed with distrust,
indeed distaste, by liberal neoclassical and post-neoclassical
economics. True, formal organization has occasionally been seen
as a reasonable governance alternative to the imperfections of
the market (Arrow 1974; Williamson 1975);[3] however, the dominant picture in economics has tended to portray bureaucracy as
an institution whose thick regulative regime impedes economic
growth and threatens individual liberty (Becker 1976; Hayek
1945, 1960).

There is undeniably something cold and unattractive in
formal relations or at least, we are prone to look upon them in
such a way (Gellner 1996). For that reason, bureaucracy has
easily been considered as one of the emblems of what may be
experienced as an alienated form of relatedness to others. 'The
reigning myth today', Sennett (1992) cogently comments, 'is that

---

3. It is interesting to observe the way the relative issues are framed in this
    tradition. Bureaucracy is deemed necessary only because the market fails.
    Without market failure, social relationships could always have been
    governed though utility maximization by the exchange of goods and
    services.

the evils of society can all be understood as evils of impersonality, alienation and coldness. The sum of these three is an ideology of intimacy . . . [that] transmutes political categories into psychological categories.' To a certain degree this is the fabrication of romanticism and of the long shadow that the predispositions it has cultivated cast over the present. The often harsh realities of pre-modern times, in which the burden of subsistence made the nowadays much praised family a predominantly economic unit, governed by severe and authoritarian patterns, are easily forgotten.[4] Modern life is surely impersonal and formal, yet in the aforementioned sense of involving a multitude of transactions (as opposed to relationships) between strangers. Transactions of this sort are about things that are not strictly personal (for example, delivering a lecture, a treatment or another service or participating in a meeting) and have therefore to be conducted and concluded in a relatively frictionless fashion. In this respect, the criticism directed against bureaucracy could indeed be seen to involve the criticism of the modern social order in its entirety, as communitarianism (Etzioni 2000) has made evident over the recent past (Armbruster 2005; Sennett 1992). Given the character of modern life, it is difficult to imagine ways of carrying out these activities in which formality is not a central feature.

Be that as it may, the understanding of bureaucracy as an institution integral to the modern social order suggests that the decline, redesign or assault on bureaucracy signals or is in any case associated with major societal changes. To a certain degree, the forces behind these changes can be seen as predominantly ideological, reflecting the neoliberal attack on the welfare state, consequent upon the historical decline of socialist ideology (Harvey 2005). The privatization and disaggregation of public organizations, deregulation and flexibilization of labour are some of the means through which the safety net of the welfare state, constructed over the course of the twentieth century, has

4.   Giddens (2000: 54) comments as follows on this subject: 'The traditional family was above all an economic unit. Agricultural production normally involved the whole family group while among the gentry and aristocracy transmission of property was the main basis of marriage. In medieval Europe, marriage was not contracted on the basis of sexual love, nor was it regarded as a place where such love should flourish. As the French historian Georges Duby, puts it, marriage in the Middle Ages was not to involve "frivolity, passion or fantasy".'

been weakened or even dismantled (Clarke 2005; Newman 2005; Reed 2005). Developments in the private sector, such as those expressed by deregulation and the decline of trade unions, could similarly be attributed to important ideological shifts (Beck 2000).

However, the sheer ideological understanding of these trends is not enough to account for their distinctive character and direction. It is necessary to look beyond ideology into the very micro-foundations of current developments that seem to be redefining the infrastructural base upon which the production of goods and services takes place. In the preceding chapters I sought to account for the modes by which the diffusion of technological information redefines products and services, dissolves and reconstructs the operations by which they are made, reframes practices of exchange and coordination, and enables new modes of communication and control, all of which seem to be having far-reaching organizational implications.[5] It would never have been possible to pursue disaggregation and networking without this thorough reorganization of the infrastructural base on which the organizational order of the twentieth century was predicated. Technological information becomes the cognitive currency, the standardized idiom, as it were, upon which a new organizational order can be built; in a way that parallels how generalized literacy and numeracy once supported the consolidation of the industrial society and its institutions (Cline-Cohen 1982; Gellner 1983: ch. 3 and 4).

The appreciation of these developments makes necessary an analysis of bureaucracy in ways that step beyond stereotypical conceptions of this central modern institution. In what follows I draw on a number of prominent social thinkers (most notably Gellner, Luhmann and Weber) to construct an account of bureaucracy that does justice to its distinctive constitution. I identify the historically unique contribution bureaucracy has made to modern life with the non-inclusive involvement of individuals in organizations (Kallinikos 2003, 2004a). Such a contribution is itself predicated upon distinctive anthropological foundations,

---

5. There are other important factors like those associated with the dominance of consumption and the culture of individualism (Baudrillard 1988; Bauman 2000; Miller 1995) that are crucially related to the distinctive character of current developments. For reasons of space I cannot deal in any detail with these highly intricate issues here.

that is, the modern conception of individuals as loose aggregates of skills and predispositions possible to mobilize in a piecemeal fashion, one that Gellner (1996) aptly captured in his term *modular man*. This is, I claim, a unique interpretation of bureaucracy that has been rendered visible within the present historical horizon, in which the non-inclusive involvement of individuals in social entities has been challenged by a variety of emerging work patterns (Beck 1992, 2000) and a host of managerial practices that target the entire personality of individuals (Casey 1999; Kallinikos 2003; Kunda 1992; Maravelias 2003). In this respect, the terms on which individuals are involved in organizations furnish the key features, the foundation upon which organizational forms are built.

In what follows I seek to reconstruct in some detail the historically unique social innovations bureaucracy has brought about. The non-inclusive involvement of individuals in organizations makes bureaucracy the first and, as yet, sole organizational form in which individuals are tied to organizations on selective, mobile and reversible terms. These terms provide, on the one hand, a standardized solution to the key problem of reconciling individual motives with collective action in ways that epitomize key values of the modern social order: freedom, equality, formality. On the other hand, they enable the bureaucratic organization to address emerging contingencies in a unique and, so far, instrumentally unmatched way. Throughout this chapter I seek to show that the non-inclusive involvement of individuals in organizations is the primary matrix of relations out of which emerge other derivative characteristics, often taken as the epitome of bureaucracy, such as standardization, formalization, specialization and centralization. Given the strong ties bureaucracy maintains with the modern social order, it is natural that the non-inclusive involvement of individuals in organizations is tied to the separate life orders of work, family and community and a variety of modern institutions that have sustained their separable character. Bureaucracy thus emerges as a central social institution, the predominant organizational form in modernity and not just one of several organizational forms. The prospect, therefore, of reconfiguring its axial principle, coinciding with the non-inclusive terms on which individuals are involved in organizations, signals an epoch-making change.

7.2 The Social Innovations of Bureaucracy

Standard sociological accounts that draw on the Weberian legacy consider bureaucracy as a major organizational form essential to the expansion of industrial capitalism, and the embedding of crucial social and economic goals or ideals such as progress, growth, meritocracy and egalitarianism. In this view, bureaucracy coincides with the advent of modernity in the way I described briefly above (Gellner 1983, 1996; Luhmann 1982, 1995; Seyer 1991).

However, a different view of bureaucracy has emerged over the years in organizational sociology and the field of organization studies. Despite acknowledging the heavy influence of Weber, such a view departs subtly yet decisively from the Weberian legacy (Clegg 1994). Such a departure is epitomized by the definition of bureaucracy in terms of a limited number of key dimensions, such as standardization, formalization, centralization and role and functional specialization.[6] The empirical variability of these dimensions produces different structural configurations, a situation that has been taken to suggest different types or profiles of bureaucracies. According to such an understanding therefore, organizations could emerge as more or less bureaucratic (Bendix 1956; Blau 1957), depending on how they scored with respect to these dimensions (Hall 1982; Pugh *et al.* 1963, 1968; Scott 1981). In other words, the higher the scores on centralization, standardization, formalization and so forth the more bureaucratic an organization is. Such an account of bureaucracy, however, leaves in suspense the key issue of what makes an organization qualify as bureaucratic in the first place. Or to put it the other way around: is there a threshold (lower limit) below which organizations are not to be considered bureaucratic? This is an issue I will return to later in this chapter.

The conception of bureaucracy in these terms has brought about a drift in the meaning of the term. Thus understood, bureaucracy is largely conceived as an organizational arrangement (a structural configuration). Therein, the indissoluble links which the bureaucratic form maintains with the modern social order are somehow obscured or made to recede into the background. Neither Blau and Bendix nor the studies of the Aston

---

6. Complexity measured as the number and connections of elements has occasionally been used as a variable too. See for example Scott (1981).

group (Pugh *et al.* 1963, 1968), undertaken in England during the 1960s and early 1970s, can be made exclusively responsible for the narrow understanding of bureaucracy that became prevalent over the years. Indeed, from the viewpoint of these scholars operating in the first decades following the Second World War, it might have been felt necessary to unpack the density of the term, and examine its empirical variability.

A reinterpretation of the studies performed within what I shall call the variable paradigm of bureaucracy suggests that the four or five dimensions used to describe the bureaucratic constitution of an organization could collapse into hierarchy and rule-bound behaviour as the epitomes of the bureaucratic form of organization. In one sense, rule-bound behaviour conveys even more than hierarchy the traditional understanding of the bureaucracy as a system of routines, rules and standard operating procedures (Perrow 1986). Rule-bound behaviour is expressed in an elaborate social edifice of rules, routines and formal role systems stipulating job positions, duties and jurisdictions and regulating interaction patterns. As a consequence, rule-bound behaviour has often been seen as the heart of the behavioural mechanics governing bureaucracy, fashioned to accommodate the functioning of modern organizations, whose operations could no longer be anchored in the normative certainty of the limited world of *Gemeinschaft*. Acting on a spatial and temporal scale, extending far beyond the limited world of pre-modern communities, modern organizations needed both legitimacy and new principles for controlling their operations, to which bureaucracy became the solution.

Formal role systems provide transparent motives and legible behaviour, essential to govern transactions between strangers or non-intimates. In the public sector, formal role systems became the basis for standardizing the delivery of public services essential to support the egalitarian and universalistic principles which public agencies embody (that is, the same services to everybody). By the same token, the imposition of a formal order in which personal goals were bracketed reflected the awareness that the pursuit of personal ends within the context of an organization may well undermine the objectives and the adequate functioning of an organization (Du Gay 1994, 2000). The standardization of expectations and action patterns that coincided with the formal order of bureaucracies were thus an essential means for avoiding haphazard initiatives and opportunism, and for improving the performance of public organizations. In the more aggressive world of industry and corporations, formal role systems and the rules and regulations with which they became associated were essential in rendering the operations of private business accountable to the state and other stakeholders. By the same token, they furnished a substantial set of restraints to the arbitrary exercise of power in the workplace (Perrow 1986) and came progressively to be formalized in the employment contract.

The social roots of bureaucracy as briefly described above are somehow obscured by its conception as a variable configuration of a limited number of dimensions. Such a conception, I suggest, altered the meaning of the term as intended by Weber. In one way or another, it became involved in blurring the qualitative differences separating bureaucracy from other organizational forms, in which individuals are involved in organizations in terms other than non-inclusive, for example custodial organizations, family businesses, pre-modern administration. It is therefore necessary to subject this view to critical scrutiny and rediscover the deep institutional roots of bureaucracy. Such a goal becomes imperative today, due to the previously described challenge that current organizational and economic developments pose to its constitutive principle. I return to this cardinal issue in the last part of this chapter. First, though, it is necessary to show in some detail how the non-inclusive involvement of individuals in organizations represents the foundation upon which bureaucracy and the organizational order of modernity are erected.

The understanding of bureaucracy solely in terms of rule-bound behaviour and hierarchy is subject to strong limitations, which emerge most clearly against the background of the highly distinctive structural principle by which the bureaucratic form came to conceive and regulate the individual–organization relationship. For the first time in history, an organizational form systematically decoupled from concrete persons the terms on which individuals were tied to organizations (Weber 1970, 1978). Supported by the wider anthropological orientations of modernity, bureaucracy dissociated people's adopted organizational roles from their social position and the experiential totality that is commonly associated with their personality or particular mode of being. It thus inaugurated a new structural principle by which individuals have come to be tied to organizations in terms other than inclusive. Non-inclusiveness implies that individuals are not contained in organizations, and organizations, in turn, are not comprised of the aggregate of persons but rather of the roles and patterns brought about by the interdependence of roles (Luhmann 1995; Tsivacou 1997). In this sense, organizations are constituted as social entities in what Luhmann (1995, 2002) calls the communicative realm; the institutionally-anchored production, reproduction and transference of distinctions.[7] The inescapable corporeality of the human condition should not be taken to imply that individuals enter organizations in their full-blown cognitive, emotional, and social complexity.

It is crucial to appreciate the distinctive status of relations out of which bureaucracy emerges as the modern form of organization. The role, not the person, constitutes the fundamental structural and behavioural element of modern formal organizing. Organizations are not made of individuals distributed over a complex landscape of job positions but of patterns built by those abstract operational requirements that we call roles. Roles are enacted by the intrinsically modern capacity of contemporary humans to suspend systematically and consistently all other personal or organizational aspects that do not bear upon the role and to undertake action along the delimited and well-specified paths prefigured by role enactment. Obviously the separation of the role from the person is a delicate and to a certain degree fragile accomplishment. By the same token, it is unmistakably present everywhere in organizations. Formal organizations would never have been viable social entities without this painstakingly acquired capacity of modern individuals to separate personal predispositions from the functional requirements and duties of the organizational role. In this sense, the living energy and the general communicative capacity of humans are essential resources for organizations (as they are for all social life) but this should not lead one to assume that formal organizations are made of individuals *qua* persons.[8]

Bureaucracy thus introduces an abstract conception of work as a set of delimited behavioural choices (duties) that can be dissociated from the totality of the life world and from every

7. For Luhmann neither organizations nor societies are substantive entities. See Luhmann (1995).
8. This view resonates with the claims advanced in Chapter 4 as regards the non-agency-centric accounts of information growth.

person's distinctive mode of being. A major objective, and an important consequence of the bureaucratic modulation of the individual–organization relationship is that individuals join the organization on the basis of considerations that relate to their ability to assume a role; that is, on the basis of merits provided by education, working experience and so on, rather than of kinship, acquaintance or other kinds of social relations. By the same token, other aspects of an individual's life are severed from bureaucratic regulation. The non-inclusive involvement of the individuals in organizations is sustained by the adequate differentiation of individual from social life and the private from the public realm. The characteristics that derive from education, professional specialization and working experience cover only a part (admittedly a very important one) of the totality of an individual's roles and social projects. In the societal context of modernity, other organizations and institutions that are clearly and unambiguously differentiated from work organizations, such as family and community, represent a crucial outlet of the individual's interests and activities. The segmentation of life into separate and relatively independent spheres is an essential requirement for the forms of human involvement upon which bureaucracy is predicated (Kallinikos 2003).

The bureaucratic form and the non-inclusive way of modulating the individual–organization relationship coincided with the gradual dissolution of class stratification and the fixed, hereditary social relations characteristic of the late feudal, early modern world (Gellner 1983, 1996; Giddens 1990; Heller 1999; Luhmann 1982, 1995, 1996). Bureaucracy emerged as the dominant modern organizational form out of the overall rational and functional preoccupations of modernity. However, the novel way of orchestrating the individual–organization relationship represented, *ipso facto*, an important vehicle for constructing a new organizational form; one premised on the ethical values of universalism and meritocracy, concordant with the bourgeois ideals of individual liberty and justice (Du Gay 2000, 2005). This new organizational order necessitated emancipation from tradition and was thus forcefully legitimated by an amalgamation of ethical and rational or functional principles. By standardizing the requirements of role performance and formalizing the process of role taking, recruitment and appointment, the bureaucratic organization became the vehicle through which jobs became potentially available to anyone who fulfilled the requirements of the job specification. It is through the very separation of the role from the person that such an availability can be rendered possible, and an employment contract signed that makes the terms of the agreement legible and enforceable at law (Weber 1947, 1970, 1978).

Bureaucracy and modernity are therefore mutually bound. Bureaucracy is the organizational form of modernity. It is closely associated with the overall cultural orientations of modern man, the social mobility that coincided with the gradual dissolution of pre-modern stratification, and the burgeoning bourgeois ideals of individual freedom and justice, which it itself helped to embed. In this respect, bureaucracy contrasts sharply with pre-modern forms of organizing that relied by and large on the principle of inclusion for regulating the relationship of people to organizations. Though present in various forms, the differentiation of personal, social and working aspects of identity was rudimentary in the agricultural, feudal world (Giddens 1991). As a consequence, these aspects of people's lives could not be separated one from another, unlike in modernity (Gellner 1983). In the pre-modern, segmented societies, the social position – defined by a fixed social stratification, generally regulated and reproduced by hereditary relations – typically determined the identity of people and their mode of (non-)subsistence. The relatively open space of bourgeois democracy and the social mobility associated with it formed the basic conditions for the emergence of the organizational form that Weber came gradually to designate as bureaucracy.

7.3 Total Organizations versus Bureaucracies

The far-reaching significance of modulating the individual–organization relationship in terms other than all-inclusive emerges clearly against the background of comparing bureaucracy with the organizational form that Goffman (1961) once called total organizations, such as mental hospitals, prisons, monasteries, army barracks or religious sects. In contrast to the non-inclusive coupling of the individual to the organization underlying bureaucracy, total organizations are based on the structural principle of inclusion. Individuals are contained in the organization; they are, in other words, inmates. Total organizations impose their austere order on the entire personality of their members. They do not distinguish between personality and collective: the term individual, as we know it, is alien to this form of organization. Total organizations thus provide an instructive contrast to bureaucracy. The latter may owe part of its administrative practices to the meticulous discipline worked out in the austere world of monasteries (Mumford 1934), yet a fathomless chasm separates the bureaucratic organization from monasteries, or other total organizations like the army, from which the bureaucratic form may have drawn significant inspiration (Morgan 1986).

The sharp distinction of bureaucracy from the inclusive and suffocating world of total organizations perhaps underplays the common normative origins of these two contrasting species of organizations, in which individual compliance to a collective purpose and unquestionable obedience or subordination to a hierarchical line of command figure prominently. The much-praised work of Foucault (1977, 1980, 1988) delivers, in bare, uncomplimentary terms, the normative origins of the modern organizational and institutional order which Foucault traces to the totalitarian practices of custodial organizations, like the prison and the mental hospital.[9] Industrial factories in early industrialism, indeed up to the end of the nineteenth century, were more custodial institutions than they were bureaucracies (Deleuze 1995; Mumford 1934, 1970). Obviously, bureaucracy as a social practice did not emerge out of the blue. The relevance which monastic life may have assumed for bureaucracy indicates that the normative order of a variety of antecedent institutions (which were more-or-less premised on the principle of inclusion) and their techniques were influential in the way formal organizations were conceived and instrumented as social entities. Weber (1978) himself attributed a central significance to the army as the functional system on which bureaucracy, especially the chain of command, was modelled (Sennett 2006).

But do these shared or, in any case, similar normative origins crowd out what at first sight would seem to be diametrically opposed modes of organization? Are the differences between a prison and a university or a bank just minor or even illusory? Within the present horizon, the comparison of these two

9. Let us be clear that Foucault did not study organizations *per se*. His investigation of the mental hospital, the clinic and the prison represent for him ways of understanding the genealogy of modern individualism and the construction of the modern individual.

opposing types of organization may be far more tricky than it would seem at first glance. If formal organizations were once influenced by the practices of total organizations, such influence has lately been reversed. Total organizations have changed substantially over the course of the last hundred years or so, as elements of the liberal ideology of modernity (rights and freedoms) joined hands with the steady development and change of professional practices (such as psychiatry, psychology or medical practice). The outcome has been a shift in both the custodial practices of total organizations and their overall social image in the direction of making their contrast to formal organizations seem less sharp.

These similarities notwithstanding, the conflation of bureaucracy with total organizations fails to distinguish between the normative order which was carried over from earlier social times and practices from the new structural principles inaugurated by bureaucracy (Gellner 1996). Structurally, bureaucracy and total organizations differ substantially in the sense of being predicated on diametrically opposed modes by which they relate to their members, that is, partial versus total inclusion. However, if the historical construction of the bureaucratic form makes it look similar to total organizations, this is due to the time-demanding and agonistic nature of social change. Structural differences like the one introduced by the non-inclusive involvement of individuals in organizations never come to pass in one blow, even though the ideologies from which they emanate may seem well established. Rather, they develop over time in tandem with the renegotiation of prevailing institutions. They disseminate themselves across the social fabric and become consolidated stepwise, and often as the outcome of social struggles that involve the gradual renegotiation of an order and the redistribution of the rights and duties of its members.

The constitutive structural principle of bureaucracy that has been embodied in the non-inclusive involvement of individuals in organizations may have been prompted initially by the irreconcilable difference between the life orders of work and civic engagement. The compartmentalization of individual life and its partial individual involvement in organizations sought to accommodate the substantially different, and in a sense diametrically opposed, character of working and civic life. That difference, perhaps traceable to the influence which the organization of the ancient Greek city-state has had on the modern polity

(Arendt 1958; Gellner 1996),[10] bespeaks the difficulties of initially reconciling the organization of work in factories or other secluded places with the liberal ideology of an open and free society. The structural principle of partial inclusion offered a solution which, being consolidated over time, allowed the ideals and practices of civic society to make their inroads into the organization of work. The diffusion of a governance regime that has been predicated on a legal–rational order and the solidification of labour rights into the employment contract gradually brought significant changes that transformed formal organizations into an entirely different species from that of total organizations. Modern discipline in institutional life presupposes the anthropological distinction of the role from the person, and the structural principle and mechanisms that embed such a distinction. Without such a separation, the objectification of one's contributions and the self-monitoring along measurable or governable dimensions would be impossible or, at least, hampered substantially. A careful reading of Foucault enhances this claim (Foucault 1977, 1980, 1988; Osborne 1994). The tangle of behaviours, orientations and techniques that constitute humans *qua* persons must be dissolved to become the target of measurement, examination and control (Hasselbladh and Kallinikos 2000; Kallinikos 1996; Townley 1994).

The profound differences separating inclusive and non-inclusive modes of regulating the individual–organization relationship are perhaps also obscured by the impressive diffusion of bureaucratic principles and the withdrawal of total organizations to the fringes of everyday modern social encounters. Being, as they are, the conventional yardstick of functional ability and institutional legitimacy, bureaucracy and the non-inclusive modulation of the individual–organization relationship tend to be taken for granted. This is indeed an indication of the degree to which bureaucracy has become part and parcel of modern life (DiMaggio 2001). However, the clear distinction of bureaucracy from total organizations and those elements of the latter that have begun to reappear over the last couple of decades make necessary the understanding of the functional efficacy of bureaucracy and its capacity to address the contingent character of modern institutional life.

10. Considerations of subsistence, since they were carried out predominantly by the slaves owned by free citizens, were not allowed to enter into political affairs in the ancient Greek city-state.

7.4 The Architecture of Complexity Revisited[11]

Despite its commonsense and, to a certain degree, justified associations with rigid and inflexible behaviour, bureaucracy is a very effective system instrumentally, with a high potential for dealing with and adapting to emerging contingencies. For structural reasons, any system with above a certain degree of complexity is bound to be drawn towards its interior, and the bureaucratic form of organization represents no exception. This is the unavoidable result of the mutual accommodation of the elements that make up the system and the interdependent character of the processes that govern its operations. Organizational closure is the inevitable outcome of system formation (Luhmann 1995). However, organizational closure does not rule out the communicative openness of the system and its ability to receive and address at least certain kinds of communicative stimuli (Cilliers 2001; Introna 1997; Tsivacou 2003). Communicative openness is relative and, like all communication, is subject to a variety of constraints.

Complex systems exemplify the tension between the need to reproduce their operations consistently through organizational closure and the demand to admit a variety of communicative inputs in order to check the relevance of these operations to the wider environment within which the system is embedded (Introna 1997; Tsivacou 2003). For instance, jobs, roles and standard operating procedures in organizations are structural elements that address the need of systems for order and efficiency. They derive only indirectly from the overall goals (production of goods or services) that the system fulfils in the wider ecology of relations within which it is embedded. While system-wide goals represent the system's means of attuning itself to its environment, these goals cannot be straightforwardly translated into jobs, roles and operating procedures (March and Simon 1993). Indeed, any immediate reference of the elements or the processes of the system directly to its external environment sets the reproduction of the system in jeop-

11. 'The Architecture of Complexity' is the title of Simon's seminal paper on the formation of complex systems and complex adaptive behaviour published initially in 1962 in *The Proceedings of the American Philosophical Society* and reprinted in his now historical volume *The Sciences of the Artificial* (1969).

ardy; it is bound to lead, sooner rather than later, to its dismantling and eventual decline (Simon 1969). In other words, system and environment are structurally and for that reason loosely coupled (Luhmann 1995). Communicative inputs enter the system via a premised interface (the relevance of the communications for the system) and are then channelled throughout the organization by means of a decision making structure that allocates the processing of these decisions to selected units and processes of the system.[12]

The friction between internal consistency and coherence versus external adaptation is the fundamental dilemma that any complex system (including the personality) confronts and which, of course, admits a variety of solutions (Weick 1979a). Much of the serious criticism directed against bureaucracy is predicated on the assumption that the bureaucratic form of organization is too inward facing, overconcerned with its own reproduction, an outcome that is closely associated with the complex edifice of rules and regulations to which internal operations must conform (Courpasson and Reed 2004; Reed 2005). Although this is true to a certain degree, this critique simplifies the conditions under which complex systems operate. Most crucially, it understates the fact that extreme concern with external contingencies and adaptability in the long run hollows out social systems (as they hollow out individuals) from the inside. Postmodern economy and culture exhibits strong tendencies towards this extreme outward directedness (Baudrillard 1988; Bauman 2000; Virilio 2000), a condition that is further aggravated by the significance information growth and dissemination tend to acquire in the contemporary world.

Bureaucracy as an institution, I suggest, plays a key role in counterbalancing some of these centrifugal trends that formal organizations confront, responding, to a certain degree, to the quest for internal coherence and consistency. At the same time, structurally, bureaucracy is a highly adaptive system. Indeed, a historical justification of bureaucracy as an organizational arrangement can be sought in its capacity to address or cope with the turbulent social, economic and technological landscape modernity has produced. It is not by accident that bureaucracy and modernity are inextricably bound together. The adaptability

---

12. Recall the analysis performed in Chapter 2 and the relevance technology plays in the construction of organizational closure.

of bureaucracy and its instrumental resilience are the straight-forward consequences of its constitutive principle: the system-atic and consistent separation of the functional requirements of the organizational system from its surrounding social and human complexity (Luhmann 1995, 1998, 2002). Let me explain further.

One of the consequences of the organizational involvement of individuals *qua* roles is the dissociation of the process of orga-nizing from the emotional, cognitive and social complexity of agents *qua* persons.[13] In contrast to persons, roles can be adapted, modified, redesigned, abandoned or reshuffled to address the emerging technical, social and economic demands the organization is facing. The bureaucratic form can thus shape and reshape the contributions of people without demanding basic changes in their personality, other than those related to atti-tudes and skill mastery. The detailed design of roles and the rules tied to their performance reflect the functional require-ments of the system, with only mild concern with what McGregor (1960) once called 'the human side of the enterprise'.[14] In this light, rule-bound behaviour is largely motivated by the project of adapting to contingent demands, rather than repro-ducing itself without consideration for these demands, as the conventional understanding of bureaucracy seems to suggest. For generally, the less an individual is emotionally attached to the role, the more flexible the invocation of the role becomes. On the other hand, emotional detachment may bring distancing and eventually indifference or estrangement. But the trade-offs between the two must be placed and evaluated within the context of the formality which modernity and the governance of formal relations make necessary.

The structural principle of non-inclusiveness establishes a

13.   This is another way of describing the reduction of complexity. By dissoci-ating organizing from the cognitive, emotional and social complexity of individuals, formal organizations narrow down the channels through which communicative stimuli enter organizational processes. It is worth remembering that for Luhmann (1995) human beings as personalities are in the environment of social systems. As a matter of fact, Luhmann's understanding of some of the key features of modernity is very distinc-tive, if not unique.

14.   For reinterpretation of what since the Hawthorn experiment has come to be called the Human Relations movement in industry, see for example, Perrow (1986) and Townley (1994).

relationship of the individual to the organization that, modulated by role formation, is marked by selectivity, mobility and reversibility (Gellner 1983, 1996; Luhmann 1982, 1995). Selectivity is the outcome of the fundamental requirement that individuals, in assuming organizational roles, are expected to suspend non-role demands, and instead act on the basis of a well-specified and delimited set of criteria that constitute the role (job description and specification, duties and jurisdictions, field of responsibility). A vast space for the development of specialized courses of action is thus opened up. The mobility in the individual–organization relationship is produced by the fact that a role, being an abstract set of functional requirements, can be untethered from the particular circumstances in which it is embedded, and be instead transferred across various organizational contexts (Hasselbladh and Kallinikos 2000).[15] Mobility is furthermore enhanced by the revocable or reversible terms of individuals' involvement in organizations. Reversibility implies that jobs can be altered or redesigned and the organizational sanctioning of job positions modified or even withdrawn, even though this may bring negative pecuniary or legal consequences. The relationship is also reversible or revocable from the point of view of the individual, who can invoke several reasons for quitting an organization, although equally, this may also bring negative pecuniary or legal consequences.

Placed against the background of these observations, bureaucracy emerges as an altogether different organizational arrangement from the conventional image that identifies it with mechanical behaviour and incapacity to change. Indeed, the demands of the current age for contingent (local and functionally adaptable), mobile and reversible (temporary) patterns of behaviour will best be satisfied by an organizational form that strengthens the bureaucratic premise, whereby individuals are tied to the organization on non-inclusive terms. Shorter time frames for organizational action, employment forms other than those implied by lifetime contracts, diffuse tasks that demand the constant redesigning of roles, virtual relations, all presuppose that individuals are coupled to organizations in terms that are characterized by selectivity, mobility and reversibility. At the historical juncture that the current age represents, bureaucracy seems to encounter its own limits, in the sense that the incessant

15. That is secretaries, accountants, supervisors and so on.

change it makes possible is undermining its own foundations (Sennett 2006).[16]

The decoupling of the organizational system from its social and human complexity provides indeed an indication of the potential such a system has for adapting to changing conditions. Through reshuffling and recombination and occasional redesign of its elements, the system gains the capacity to address emerging situations that may demand responses different from those the system has produced previously. Despite the many constraints that may be thought to underlie the re-engineering of tasks and their combinability (Kallinikos 1996, 1998a), a variety of options become available that may give the organization a broad repertoire of structural and behavioural options. The quest for flexibility cannot therefore be addressed in a genuine fashion unless contemporary forms of organization are built on the very foundations of bureaucracy as outlined here. Only by being able to reassemble the standardized elements (tasks, jobs and positions) that make up its operational infrastructure and revising its procedures to produce novel outcomes (new products, services, action patterns and so on), can an organization hope to cope with the constant eruption of contingencies. A prerequisite for doing this is to tie individuals to the organization in selective, mobile and reversible forms.

It should be clear by now that the organizational involvement of humans *qua* roles makes bureaucracy capable of unleashing the process of organizing from the inescapable context-embeddedness of the human body and the intractable (from the instrumental point of view) complexity of experiences that underlie human beings *qua* persons. Dubious as it may seem from a psychological or anthropological point of view (I intend the term philosophically), such a project is not motivated by functional considerations alone. It is inevitably tied to and ethically supported by the formal character of modern life and the nature of bureaucracy as an institution for governing formal social relations, as described in the first section of this chapter. In dissociating persons from roles, bureaucracy sets the requirements for a form of organization free from the restricted mobility of the human body and the slow process of personal and psychological reorientation. Bureaucracy's abstract principles of organization provide, indeed, the generative matrix out of which what

16.   See the preceding two chapters and the final section in this chapter.

we today call virtual relations are emerging. Virtual organization is itself contained as a germ in the very separation of the role from the person, and the design and enactment of action patterns that are only loosely coupled to the corporeality and psychological complexity of humans (Baudrillard 1983, 1988; Heller 1999; Kallinikos 1996).

The extent to which organizational and social roles can be severely decoupled from the totality that makes the distinctive mode of being of every human remains a highly delicate issue (Mangham 1995; Tsivacou 1997, 2003). However, both bureaucracy and modern society have been built on the premise that such a severe or adequate separation is possible (Gellner 1983, 1996; Luhmann 1995). Indeed, modern life provides ample evidence of the realism or, perhaps more correctly, the reality of that premise. There are undeniably human and social costs, some of them very high, from the demand for constant skill updatability and adaptability, characteristic of the contemporary world (Sennett 2000, 2006). However, it is not bureaucracy that produces that demand, even though partial inclusion as a constitutive principle could partly be credited for the ceaseless role re-engineering and frequent updatability of skills that are taking place in organizations these days. Yet these processes occur and are, to a certain degree, driven by the character of contemporary life and the orientation of current societies towards limitless economic growth and expanding consumption (Castoriadis 1987). Placed in this context, bureaucracy emerges indeed as innocent while its relative structural stability and institutional embeddedness seem to offer a counter force to the uprooting 'culture of new capitalism' (Sennett 2000, 2006).

To conclude this section, it seems necessary to deliver, very briefly, a few observations on what many people tend to consider as counter evidence to the claim of the adequate separation of the person from the role; namely the diffusion of what has over the last two or three decades come to be called Human Resource Management (HRM).[17] It would seem perhaps reasonable to conjecture that as far as HRM targets the individual as a psychological unity it challenges the constitutive principle of partial inclusion and the clear-cut separation of the role from the

---

17. A distinction should be made between Organizational Behaviour and HRM. The first is an academic discipline, the second a bundle of techniques aiming at providing vocational training.

person. However, the body of practices and second-hand psychological knowledge that make up HRM do not deal with individuals conceived as anthropological totalities. To believe it does so is to fall victim to a deception. HRM is rather concerned with what I would call the management of the interface between the role and the individual, with the purpose of minimizing the friction and making the frequent transitions from the person to the role as smooth as possible (Kallinikos 2003). As its name reveals, it is concerned with humans conceived as resources and with the management of these resources: skill availability, organizational demographics, reward systems and the rest. All the metrics and techniques it has developed over the years provide ample evidence of its fundamental instrumental orientation (Townley 1994). If anything, the development and diffusion of HRM is a clear manifestation that the separation of the role from the person has acquired massive dimensions that need to be managed.[18]

7.5   Defining the Modern Structural Template

As construed here, bureaucracy as an organizational form coincides with the non-inclusive terms by which individuals are involved in the organizational system. A number of far-reaching ethical and functional implications ensue from this historically unique way of conceiving and modulating the relationship between individual motives and collective action. However, in such an account of bureaucracy, it is not entirely clear how that ubiquitous attribute of formal organizations, hierarchical constitution, fits into the whole picture. One of the key criticisms raised against bureaucracy is that the frequent hierarchical mediation of many decisions makes this organizational form too cumbersome, limiting individual autonomy and inhibiting the responsiveness of the organization to the demands it faces.

The pervasive trans-cultural and trans-historical nature of

18.   A more sinister explanation of HRM would be to consider it as one of the means for allowing work and professional concerns to expand at the expense of the variety of interests and preoccupations that the modern self and the adequate separation of the life orders of family, work and civic life once entertained. See Kallinikos (2003) and Sennett (2000, 2006). In this sense, HRM does participate in the weakening of the sharp differences separating work from other life orders. For a different view see Rose (1999), Kunda (1992) and Maravelias (2003).

hierarchy suggests that hierarchical stratification is not limited to bureaucracy (Dumont 1970). Hierarchy cannot thus be exclusively attributed to bureaucracy, a claim that is reinforced by the fact that in modern society bureaucracy is far from the only institution to be governed by hierarchy. Most crucially perhaps, to attribute to the bureaucratic form of organization an invariable degree of centralization entails, as I will demonstrate below, too strong a generalization and one that, further, is not supported by the empirical findings of the aforementioned variable paradigm on bureaucracy. What seems indeed to be distinctive in the hierarchical configuration of bureaucratic organization is the relatively clear and rule-bound regulation of the exercise of power, as distinct from the exercise of arbitrary rule or the predominantly normative mediation of rule in traditional societies. In bureaucracies, the jurisdictional domain of power is delimited and relatively well specified while its exercise is governed by rules, constituting what, after Weber (1947), is referred to as rational–legal authority (juxtaposed with charismatic and traditional authority). The delimited object domain and rule-bound regulation of authority is closely associated with the selective, mobile and reversible terms of modulating the individual–organization relationship. Authority is tied to the office or the role and is exercised upon a specific domain of organizational operations, while its organizational sanctioning can be withdrawn at any moment.

It is reasonable to assume that the edifice of rules and regulations that govern the exercise of authority in formal organizations and other aspects of an organization's operations may have produced a more fine-grained hierarchical stratification than would otherwise have been the case (Hall 1982). In this respect, the recent relaxation of part of the rules and regulations involved in the governance of formal organizations (as the result of the trends described in the preceding chapters) may have made its contribution to the de-layering of organizations that has been observed over the last two decades or so. However, an inevitable outcome of these trends is the indirect reintroduction of the exercise of arbitrary rule created by the looser regulation of power. There are many stakes behind the verbal cosmetics of decentralization and the prevailing managerial rhetoric.

Be that as it may, the claim concerning the limited adaptability of the bureaucratic form caused by centralised rule could make sense against the background of the tacit assumption that bureaucracy is governed by a high and largely invariable degree of centralization. However, the development and diversity of the modern organizational landscape tells another story. Centralization shows a highly variable degree throughout the history of industrialism and modernity (Chandler 1977) and across the highly differentiated contexts underlying it (Blau 1957). The results of the empirical studies carried out by what I called earlier the variable paradigm suggest that the degree of centralization is subject to variation, dependent on the instrumental and environmental conditions facing an organization (Burns and Stalker 1961; Galbraith 1973; Hage and Aiken 1969; Pugh *et al*. 1963, 1968; Scott 1981). The variability of centralization that formal organizations exhibit indicates that it may be difficult to define the distribution of the loci of decisions (Tsoukas 1996) as the sole criterion for the alleged historical decline of bureaucracy and the emergence of alternative forms of organization, ones simply marked by lower degrees of centralization.

The same holds true for the other key dimensions of standardization, formalization, and task and role specialization. None of these dimensions can be made the yardstick for deciding the key issue of what makes an organization conform to the bureaucratic form or not. Is it really possible to decide *a priori* and investigate empirically the threshold beyond which these dimensions suggest an organization to be an instance of the bureaucratic form? This seems to me to be a futile project. Organizations may score differently on these dimensions but it is not possible to provide by these means a decisive test of whether an organization is or is not a bureaucracy. The decisive test must therefore be sought elsewhere, that is, in the terms by which the fundamental issue of the relationship between the individual and the organization is addressed. The non-inclusive involvement of individuals in organizations provides the unmistakable criterion for deciding whether an organization is an instance of the bureaucratic form or not. The alternatives to bureaucracy have the form of the total organization or of small, kinship-based firms (such as family businesses) in which the distinctive line between work and the rest of an individual's life is blurred.[19]

---

19. Traditional organizations (most agricultural) based on serfdom and patronage or pre-modern administrative systems in which the concept of employee as it is known to us did not exist provide historical examples of other organizational forms (Gellner 1983, 1996).

The historical development of the non-inclusive involvement of individuals in organizations seems to suggest that the bureaucratic form is the outcome of a choice that, by now, exhibits binary qualities (Kallinikos 1998a; Luhmann 1995; Tsivacou 1997). The terms by which individuals are involved in organizations are either inclusive or non-inclusive. It is inconsistent and contradictory to have both. It would be possible to have different modes regulating the individual involvement in separate subsystems of an organization, but each subsystem can only be regulated by one mode. I referred above to total organizations that regulate the life of inmates through an inclusive, non-modular relationship. However, administration in, say, prisons or mental hospitals is organized according to non-inclusive, modular relationships and administrative staff occupy and enact distinctive roles. The selection of either of the two alternatives provides the premises upon which very distinctive organizational forms emerge. By contrast to this binary choice, characteristics like standardization and centralization exhibit a graded intensity. It is always possible to have less or more standardization or centralization. In this sense neither of these characteristics can become the ultimate arbiter for deciding whether an organization represents an instance of the bureaucratic form or not.

Therefore, no matter how important they may be in other respects, the dimensions of centralization, standardization, formalization and specialization develop within the constitutive framework of relations established by the non-inclusive forms of human involvement and the selective, mobile and reversible terms by which individuals are tied to organizations. These terms provide the very foundation of the bureaucratic organization. They constitute the primary relation out of which other secondary or derivative characteristics emerge. It is crucial to uphold the distinction between primary and derivative characteristics. Routines, standard operating procedures and centralization, while undeniably important, are derivative characteristics of the bureaucratic organization. They emerge upon the very foundation established by the clear separation of the individual from the organization, and the selective, mobile and reversible terms by which individuals are tied to organizations.

What about the claim then of an age of post-bureaucracy? Do not some of the socioeconomic developments mentioned in this chapter and described in some detail throughout this volume lead to the modification of the standard structural template with which bureaucracy has been identified? While unclear and variously deployed (Casey 2004; DiMaggio 2001; Heckscher and Donnellon 1994; Hodgson 2004), the term post-bureaucracy suggests a qualified discontinuity with the past. Post-bureaucratic organizations represent examples of a systematic modification of the standard structural template of bureaucracy and some of its practices but they do not break with the core of what has constituted the bureaucratic form of organization. However, it is unclear how this core is defined in the current literature on post-bureaucracy. The tacit assumption that can be made by reading this literature is that centralization, routines and standard operating procedures represent the essence of bureaucracy. As I have been at pains to show here, the existence of rules and regulations alone and/or the degree of centralization do not suffice to define the bureaucratic form. Indeed, as Thompson and Alvesson (2005) show in their review of the empirical literature on post-bureaucracy, rules and regulations in organizations have proliferated rather than diminished over the last two or three decades. The distinctive character of bureaucracy should therefore be sought elsewhere. Whether post-bureaucracies involve merely a modification of the regulative regime of modern bureaucracy or its radical transformation can only be decided by the close investigation of the terms on which individuals are involved in organizations.

7.6 Concluding Remarks on Modernity and Bureaucracy

The account of bureaucracy that has been put forth in this chapter undeniably involves a broad interpretation as to what counts as bureaucracy. In the final analysis, it tends to identify modernity with bureaucracy. A clear consequence of such an interpretation is to regard the overwhelming majority of formal organizations as instances of the bureaucratic form, differing only in terms of a number of secondary characteristics such as standardization and centralization.

Broad as it may be, the account of bureaucracy advanced in this chapter is triggered by the alleged prospect of its decline at the current historical juncture that seems to entail the global re-evaluation of modernity and certain of its key characteristics. An interpretation of bureaucracy in the broad terms that I have attempted here would presumably have been irrelevant under other conditions, ones that did not challenge its constitutive principle. It does not seem to me an accident, therefore, that such an interpretation has not previously been sought. It is the assumption or proclamation of the conclusion of an age that, along with the decline of its basic forms of organization, inevitably prompts the examination of the very foundations on which the organizational order of modernity rests. The present chapter sought to address these cardinal issues. This re-excavation of the forgotten foundations of the organizational order of modernity pursued here suggests that only a substantial redefinition of the core, constitutive properties of bureaucracy can really break with the institutional principles that bureaucracy embodies and embeds. Only the radical redefinition of the non-inclusive forms of human involvement in organizations can lead to a new organizational order and a new society.

Three current developments seem to me to represent indicators of the trend away from the bureaucratic form that has dominated the modern industrial order. The first of them coincides with the deregulation of the institutional base for the exercise of rule in organizations, manifested in looser forms of accountability and less restrictive employment law.[20] Deregulation has so far kept intact the core constitutive principle of bureaucracy but it has reintroduced into the governance of formal organizations elements of normative regulation as opposed to the predominantly rational–legal regime decreeing the bureaucratic order. The developments deregulation is associated with may well reflect the historical victory of capital over labour, the decline of labour unions and the effects of globalization (Harvey 2005). Obviously, the substantial redefinition of the regimes that govern the various forms of corporate accountability is bound to change formal organizations as they have been known to us considerably. Extensive deregulation will come in the long run to furnish the premises for the radical revision and perhaps abandonment of one of the most salient features of modernity, the employment contract (Sennett 2006).

20. Interestingly, in a relatively recent article following the Enron case, *The Economist* suggested that the enhancement of bureaucracy seems to be a necessary development to avoid similar cases in the future. However, this is a very restrictive understanding of the broad scope of the organizational form of bureaucracy. See Du Gay (2005: 2).

The second trend that challenges bureaucracy and the organizational order of modernity coincides with the flexibilization of labour and the diffusion of alternative forms of work (Barley and Kunda 2004; Evans *et al.* 2004). These trends seem to have a double-edged character. On the one hand, they accentuate some of the intrinsic characteristics of the modern bureaucratic form, making selectivity, mobility and reversibility even more pronounced than they have been until quite recently. Contingent work is the most typical case of these trends which, if considerably diffused, may lead to what Beck (2000) described as the Brazilianization of Europe. These kind of effects which the flexibilization of work brings about, are somewhat self-ironic, in the sense of involving the travesty of bureaucracy's constitutive principle as I have described it in this chapter. There are obviously limits to the selective, mobile and reversible modes of individual involvement in organizations. On the other hand, the flexibilization of labour opens the road to the normative as opposed to the legal–rational regulation of work and the involvement of individuals in organizations in terms that lead to a certain re-traditionalization of the forms of governing organizations (Kunda 1992).

Re-traditionalization is the combined effect of the deregulation and flexibilization of labour. It most clearly, I think, challenges the bureaucratic form by straightforwardly questioning its constitutive principle of the non-inclusive involvement of individuals in organizations. A number of social and managerial practices have developed over the last two decades that seek to involve individuals in organizations in terms that tend to blur the modern distinction between working or professional and personal life (Casey 1999; Kallinikos 2003; Kunda 1992). Organizations reclaim not only the skills but the soul of their employees. The demands for a successful professional life have often taken dimensions that increasingly squeeze the opportunities left for other personal and civic engagements (Sennett 2000, 2006). Family becomes a burden to professional development (especially for women) while crucial personal characteristics like sexual appeal and attractiveness, reserved once predominantly for the realm of intimacy, are increasingly, and most crucially systematically, brought to bear on the accomplishment of organizational objectives. Long hours of work further weaken an already fragile community and public life (Murray *et al.* 2002). The predominantly normative regulation of individual involvement in organizations blurs the boundaries of the institutional separation of work, family and community that sustained the non-inclusive involvement of individuals in organizations (Carnoy 2000; Kallinikos 2003; Sennett 2000, 2006). Elements reminiscent of the inclusive forms of human involvement in organizations re-emerge out of a past that seemed distant and parochial only two decades ago. Perhaps the organizational forms and work practices of late or post-modernity will involve combinations that seemed impossible, unthinkable or inconsequential from the horizon of high modernity.

8. Epilogue on Technology and Institutions

8.1 Computational Rendition of Reality

The organizational patterns of modernity and the institutions that have supported it are undergoing a significant transformation. In this volume, I have sought to explore the nature of this transformation by tracing certain of the driving forces that underpin it to the comprehensive infrastructural changes that are brought about by the expanding organizational involvement of the new information and communication technologies. Technological processes may at first glance seem at a remove from the institutional context that has supported the organizational order of modernity. However, the organization of modern society has been inextricably bound up with a variety of objectifying modes and strategies (Arendt 1958; Kallinikos 1996) of which technology has been an integral part. Technology and objectification are but two sides of the same coin (Heidegger 1977).[1] An impressive array of operations across organizations and institutional settings has been instrumented and sustained by means of technological processes. The involvement of technology in organizations is so thorough that the pattern of interactions it gives rise to defies interpretation in terms of a straightforward instrumental logic that considers technology as just a means to pre-established ends.

1. This point is forcefully made by Heidegger (1977) in his essay *The Age of the World Picture* and more specifically in the footnotes appended to that essay in which he discusses the cardinal role played in this process by the understanding of 'what is' as something projected and put against – *vorstellen*. Unfortunately the term *Vorstellung* has been translated into English as *representation*, which is one of its predominant current meanings in German. Yet the German term still retains strong ties to its original connotation of 'something put against' which tends to be lost in the English translation. Indeed, the term stands much closer to the Latin *obicere* (to throw against), from which objectification derives (Arendt 1958: 137).

The technological developments of information growth, which have been triggered by the deepening involvement of the computational paradigm in all walks of life, have transformed information from simply a means for planning and carrying out a variety of operations to a comprehensive platform for framing, instrumenting and acting upon the world. Substantial portions of reality are currently perceived and mediated through access to technological information and manipulated by means of a steadily interlocking ecology of information and communication technologies. Technological information, I have claimed, has been centrally implicated in the creation of a pervading instrumental habitat that has been changing, slowly but profoundly, the conditions under which economic agents and organizations operate. In gathering momentum, these developments have come to exercise strong pressures upon the organizational and economic arrangements that have prevailed over the last century and the institutional web of relations within which these arrangements have been embedded.

The implications that are associated with the growing significance of technological information could be summarized along three axes: changes in work processes and structural mechanisms associated with the penetration of organizations by technological information; the reconstitution of the heterogeneous nature of reality as permutable information and its effect on monitoring and control of collective effort; and new modes of action and control at a distance.

The first cluster of changes are closely associated with the deep penetration of organizations by technological information. This has led to the extensive automation of production and administration, and the consequent reparsing and reconstitution of a significant number of organizational tasks and operations. Over the past few decades, the transformation of the task infrastructure of organizations has resulted in the establishment of new organizational processes and procedures and the creation of new services that, in turn, have brought about one of several modes of functional and structural accommodation. Administrative simplification, flatter hierarchies, better cross-functional or cross-agency communication and improved responsiveness to environmental contingencies represent examples of the kind of changes associated with the informatized rendition of organizational tasks and operations. Overall, this cluster of changes seem to have, by and large, continued the

industrial tradition of deploying technology as an important
means for work and administrative rationalization (Yates and
Van Maanen 2001; Zuboff 1988) but in the new forms computer-
based technologies have made possible.[2]

The most significant organizational transformation with serious institutional repercussions comes from a second cluster of
developments that differ substantially from the project of
automation and rationalization, if not by intention at least in
terms of their implications. Throughout this volume, I have associated these developments with the growing dissolvability of the
elementary and compact micro-texture of organizational operations, consequent upon the extensive rendition of the task infrastructure of organizations as technological information. Human
involvement in the world has traditionally been bound up with
the enduring shape of reality, as it is comprised by the concrete,
tangible, standing-apart and observable character of things and
their interrelationships.[3] In particular, the history of work is, to a
considerable degree, a protracted effort to deal with and master
the recalcitrant materiality and tangibility of the world. To work
has always meant to be immersed in the materiality of the world,
acting upon and transforming the physical character of things,
as they are presented to immediate perception and bodily
dexterity or sensibility (Arendt 1958; Zuboff 1988).[4] The extensive partition of the world, brought about by a deepening division of labour in the recent history of industrial capitalism,
seldom moved beyond the extendability and presentability of
materials and things (Flusser 2000, 2003).

Technological information produced by means of computation breaks with this primordial human dependence on the
extendible and presentable character of the world, and the tangibility and corporeality of labour. It penetrates beyond the shape
of things, in the unobservable substratum by which they are
made (or are assumed to be made) and reconstructs them by
recourse to operations (computations) that elude human embeddedness in the world and the inexorable tangible/situated character of work (Flusser 2003). Due to its analytic predilection,

2. See Chapters 2 and 5.
3. I make a distinction here between action, on one hand, and contempla-
tion/imagination, on the other (see Arendt 1958).
4. *The Capital* (Marx 1954, 1956) still stands as one of the most fascinating
descriptions of the material character of work that we have yet.

cognition has, long before the advent of computation, been inevitably involved in the partition and itemization of the world. Especially in the form of scientific work, cognition has always sought to penetrate beyond the observable and given, and reconstruct the world through its unobservable correlates and processes (scientific abstraction), many of which have been assumed to develop beneath the enduring shapes of a solid reality. Some of the abstractions of science have reached down into the material character of work through the extensive involvement of industrial technology in the accomplishment and monitoring of work processes. The analytic predilection of cognition has furthermore crept into the everyday life of organizations in the mundane medium of administration; as an instance of cognitive work, administration signifies a step away from involvement with the materiality of the world. Administrative processes are inevitably entangled with analytical categories, abstractions, numerical systems and technical notation, and other modes of ordering and calculation by means of which the monitoring and control of collective human effort take place (Cline-Cohen 1982; Kallinikos 1996; Rose 1999; Zuboff 1988).

Computation and technological information continue this tradition of cognitive analysability. They give it, though, an interesting shift and endow it with a momentum that would have been unimaginable without recourse to the formidable processing capacity of contemporary technology of computing and the reconstruction of the world as a huge series of binary computations. As I have been at pains to show in Chapters 2, 3 and 5, technological information pierces deep into the microscopic texture of many tasks and operations, far beyond the observable extendability and complexion of things. To use figurative language, if industrial technology advanced the itemization of the world, computation is currently involved in its pulverization (Flusser 2003). This is the inevitable outcome of the binary constitution of computation and the logistic, cognitive and analytic nature of software engineering and programming. By being rendered as information by computational means, tasks are meticulously broken down into minute steps and reconstructed through the chained operations that constitute programs. The operation of programs themselves needs be sustained by other software that pierces even further into the invisible constitution of reality and so forth. The information that reaches the interface with human agents is just the final step of a huge series of other automated information processing operations taking place below.[5] These developments elude immediate observation and must often be retraced and reconstructed analytically (Hayles 2005; Kittler 1997). Perhaps this is a reason why the relevant processes have not, as yet, been appreciated in their seriousness and depth. They have also been overlooked because social scientists are often not, or not sufficiently, technically able to understand the complexity of these processes.

The instrumental consequences of the growing dissolvability of organizational tasks and operations, as the outcome of the computational rendition of reality, are far-reaching. Dissolvability discloses another face of reality, ready to be manipulated, and leads accordingly to the functional recomposition of tasks and operations and their spatial and interorganizational redistribution. The much-noted overcoming of the geographical embeddedness of production and administration associated with information and communication technologies is, to a significant degree, the outcome of these processes. The recomposition of reality as a computed order is furthermore crucially involved in the establishment of new organizational, regional and global architectures of control, in which access to, and capacity to act upon and manipulate information figure prominently (Sassen 2001). A new instrumental habitat keeps on forming around these trends. Large, growing and interoperable information infrastructures are taking shape as computational reduction overcomes the intrinsic heterogeneity and the often irreconcilable differences of the varying domains of the real. An increasing variety of information sources are brought to bear upon one another, and will increasingly do so in the future, as the outcome of this reconstitution of the intrinsically heterogeneous character of reality as permutable information.[6]

The third group of instrumental implications are associated with new forms of communication and control which the interoperable universe of information and communication technologies make possible. The lower cost of communication, the speed by which technological information can be exchanged and,

---

5.   I am not referring here to nanotechnology, though the discovery and technological reconstruction of nano-processes is intimately related to computation and the drift away from the tangibility and observability of the world.
6.   See Chapters 2 and 3.

perhaps most importantly, the variety, precision and richness of the exchanged information, all provide new opportunities for coordination, action and control at a distance. The organizational and economic implications of these new forms of communication have been noticed in the literature and widely discussed.[7] Seldom have they, however, been related to the computational reconstitution of reality or to the interoperable ecology of information and communication technologies which computation ultimately makes possible. Important as it may be, communication is a second-order effect emanating from the computational technology's capacity to recapture and render a variety of tasks and operations as data and information items. If the capturing of reality once involved the conquest of space, the extension of the world is currently explored through another and to a certain degree counter-intuitive route that entails capturing the elementary microscopic fabric of life.[8]

8.2   Structural and Institutional Implications

As a precis of an important part of this volume, the preceding section suggests that the computational rendition of an expanding range of economic and organizational tasks and operations makes them increasingly mobile and transferable across settings. Computation is also crucially implicated in the construction of extended zones of interoperability, in which technological data and information produced under vastly shifting circumstances can intersect and be recombined in a variety of ways. Rendered as information, reality is made pliable and manipulable (Borgmann 1999). A few key organizational and institutional implications are tied to this growing instrumental significance of information which I sought to analyse in the second part of this volume, mainly Chapters 5, 6 and 7.

New modes of organizing and coordinating human effort,

---

7. See Chapters 2 and 5.
8. Flusser (2000) suggests that strong affinities underlie the microscopic orientation of computation, genetic biology and quark physics and their movement away from *res extensa*. This brings to mind those shifts in thought sensibilities which Foucault (1970) analysed in his masterpiece *The Order of Things*. Only a man with the erudition and imagination of Foucault could, perhaps, undertake the analogous and gigantic intellectual task of tracing the 'archaeological' origins of computation, genetic biology and contemporary physics.

commonly referred to as networks,[9] seek to accommodate the growing independence from location and fixed assets which the rendering of reality as information offers. Computational reduction and dissolvability allow for the disaggregation of bundled operations and their recomposition in ways that draw advantage from the skewed organizational and geographical distribution of skills, resources and opportunities. Certainly, the history of industrial capitalism, and the organizational arrangements it has generated, can be read as a progressive emancipation of the constraints associated with the material and inescapable local embeddedness of production and administration (Fligstein 1990; Kallinikos 1996; Zuboff 1988). Over the course of industrial capitalism, the mobility, transferability and combinability of resources used in production have steadily risen, while a deepening division of labour has produced a fine-grained functional and structural differentiation of organizations (Castells 1996; Fligstein 1990; Chandler 1977). In particular, the structural separation of non-management functions from production functions, consequent upon the deep functional differentiation of these groups of operations, has constituted an important precedent for the disaggregating trends of organizations that have been observed over the last two decades or so. The emerging organizational arrangements of producing and distributing goods and services that networks exemplify therefore draw heavily on the established division of labour and the structural and functional differentiation of organizations. Nevertheless, the instrumental involvement and significance of technological information give the functional and structural differentiation of organizations, and the division of labour on which it rests, new momentum.

In this respect, networks challenge formal organizations as organizational arrangements (as tightly composed functional assemblages) that have predominantly been based on boundedness and unified hierarchical command. However, formal organizations, as I have claimed throughout this volume, are not just functional arrangements but complex imbrications of structural–functional and institutional elements. While it can be thought possible to engineer structural and functional change or

9.　I have grown increasingly suspicious about the use of the term 'network'. On the other hand the term is now well established and it seems indeed difficult to find a credible alternative.

account for them on the basis of rational considerations (which often turn out to be no more than rationalized beliefs) alone, institutional reformation is a much more complex and slow process. It involves the renegotiation of an established order on the basis of matters that transcend the limited cosmological horizon of rationality. Formal organizations are not just functional arrangements geared to maximizing output, but complex, historical constructions closely associated with the modern social order, the governance of formal relations (relations between non-intimates), the establishment of rights and obligations (for example, property rights or the labour contract) and a variety of legally-embedded forms of accountability (Fligstein 2001; Kallinikos 2004a). The fact that networks are variously constrained by the prevailing institutional order is shown in the ferment of institutional reform that has, over the last two or three decades, come to be known as deregulation. The ardent quest to revise significant areas of the established framework of rules, laws and regulations is intimately tied to the perception of benefits and the new architectures of control, which the hyper-mobility of resources, associated with the technological informatization of reality, makes possible.

A crucial target of the struggle to reconstruct some of the institutional foundations on which formal organizations rest entails the revision of the forms of individual involvement in organizations that have, conventionally, been regulated by the employment contract. Despite the fact that I have not focused explicitly on the labour contract in this volume, I attribute a central significance to it, nonetheless. The employment or labour contract is the legal–institutional expression of a profound historical accomplishment that coincides with the non-inclusive involvement of individuals in organizations. The bureaucratic constitution of formal organizations, as I have been at pains to show in this volume, is predicated upon the partial involvement of individuals in organizations. A number of crucial goals are fulfilled this way which I described in some detail in the preceding two chapters. Firstly, work is delimited against the larger background of social and civic life and governed through a specific regime of rules and regulations, which to a considerable degree reflect the overall liberal orientation of the modern, democratic social order. Secondly, by sufficiently demarcating work from the rest of an individual's projects, the partial involvement of individuals in organizations contributes to the social embeddedness of the distinct character of the life domains of work, family and community. No one of these domains is, or should be, reducible and subordinated to another, even though work is variously implicated in the social status of individuals. Thirdly, formal organizations become a key instrument for managing social encounters and transactions between non-intimates, in a fairly predictable and smooth way that establishes civility, combats discrimination and guarantees the accessibility of basic social or collective goods and services for everybody. Fourthly, by decoupling the governance of formal organizations from individuals, *qua* persons, organizations become able to reshuffle and recombine roles, tasks and procedures in ways that neither depend nor impinge directly upon the anthropological totality of the individual as a person. Individuals and organizations are rendered, to use a now widely-diffused terminology, loosely coupled, and organizations thus obtain a functional ability and flexibility that would otherwise have been substantially hampered.

The picture of change into which the diffusion of technological information is embedded is therefore much bigger and more complex than usually seems to be the case when networks and, particularly, formal organizations are considered as just structural and functional assemblages. Contemplating the deep embeddedness of formal organizations and bureaucracy in modern life, one cannot but look upon current developments with ambiguous and, to a certain degree, conservative feelings. The implications of some of these changes for democracy and the social order, in which we have been living over the last fifty years, may be, as Tilly (2001) suggests, 'chilling'.[10] On the other hand, it is difficult to envisage a reversal or even a slowing down of the developments associated with the march of technological information: quite the opposite. As I have claimed in Chapter 3 and empirical data demonstrates, technological information will continue to expand, most probably at an accelerating pace.[11] New technological developments make data and information produced for an amazing variety of purposes interoperable and simultaneously short-lived and disposable. If I am right on this point, then the continuing growth of information will come to change the texture of social, economic and institutional life

10.   See Chapter 6 for more details on these issues.
11.   See the report by Lyman *et al.*, *How Much Information* (2003) and the Appendix of this volume.

considerably. The precise forms of this change are not clear but I have sought in this volume to focus on and analyse some of the implications these developments may have. An interpretation of past experience suggests that the nearly escalating growth of information is bound to exercise a pressure upon the established web of institutional relations to accommodate the individual, economic and organizational appropriation, use and dissemination of information.[12] As always, perhaps, the ultimate outcome will be a compromise between future possibility and current actuality.

12. The organization and the forms of information dissemination are key issues (Introna and Nissenbaum 2000) that are bound to become even more crucial in the future, as information penetrates deeper into the textures of institutional and personal life.

Appendix: Indicators and Patterns of Information Growth[1]

There are various indicators that could be used to measure the continuous growth of information. Most of these indicators have the status of proxies that are easily depreciable due to the rapid character of change underlying the phenomena they seek to capture. It is, therefore, the trends that we would like to emphasize here and not the absolute numbers used to produce some of the following graphical representations. In addition to being easily depreciable, proxies for measuring characteristics of complex infrastructures (like the internet) are themselves very much contingent upon the methodology that is used to carry out the measurement. Trends are by definition more time-persisting and the identification of trends could thus be said to offer somewhat more reliable indicators of information growth.

According to a study carried out from Berkeley entitled *How Much Information*,[2] already referred to in Chapter 3, a distinction is being made between what is termed the surface versus the deep web (Figure A1). Whereas the surface web can be defined as what is publicly available in fixed web pages, it becomes evident that behind it rests a much deeper and more complex information infrastructure that not only supports the surface web by a variety of technological means but also informs its content through database-driven processes. This is roughly what is indicated by the term *deep web*. It is important however to understand that this process is not unilateral. The surface web can be seen as the platform that facilitates the interaction between itself and internet users with direct implications for the deep web that feeds back to the surface web. The 'updating' of the deep web partly occurs via the surface web as transactions taking place between users and the surface web are 'transferred'

1. Prepared by Dionysios Demetis (http://www.demetis.com) and Jannis Kallinikos.
2. http://www.sims.berkeley.edu/research/projects/how-much-info-2003/

to the databases of the deep web. The growth of the surface web, in turn, is reflected back to the growth and organization of the deep web as new data and information are needed to support the development of new services that are mediated by the surface web.

In systems terminology one can describe such interdependence as interpenetration and structural coupling.[3] It is undeniably true that there are a number of databases that could be classified as part of the deep web and which are not accessible via the surface web. However, the driving force that pushes the increased interpenetration of the deep and the surface web is irresistible in an information age that marches at a phenomenal pace. Even government is now on board to exploit the advances of technology and the internet, hence transforming itself into e-government and providing a variety of means by which citizens can interact with traditional structures like tax authorities and voting.

Before we move on to describe some proxies that indicate increased internet usage, it is vital that we differentiate conceptually between the surface web and the deep web through an example. At the same time however, we recognize that the issue of structural coupling between the two and its significance for information processing and growth is something that deserves further pondering and research and hence we do not expect to resolve this matter here. We just introduce the difference and exemplify it for illustrative purposes. Let us take the example of a bank through one mode of interaction alone, namely that of online banking.

Even though there are clearly other modes of interactions (ATM, telephone banking or simply physically carrying out a transaction in a bank branch), all such interactions affect the deep web, that is, the underlying databases within which the totality of a bank's recorded transactions reside. The example provided here denotes interactions of several users with the surface web via personal computers[4] and through the bank's fixed web page (that is, www.thenameofthebank.com). An important distinction needs to be made here. Information growth occurs regardless of the mode of interaction between user and system, hence the deep web constantly deepens. However, we argue that interactions

3. See Luhmann (1995).
4. There are other ways that this process can be facilitated (for example, through mobile phones, PDAs, and so on.)

Figure A.1   Surface Web and Deep Web

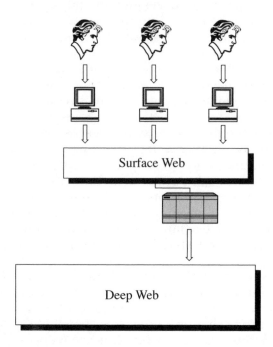

through the internet are likely to become the predominant mode of interaction through which information growth and the deepening of the web will be realized (given the phenomenal growth of the latter and the indicators we discuss below). Furthermore, such deepening of the deep web (a self-referential process analysed in Chapter 3) affects the surface web through a multiplicity of ways. Through the surface web, the deep web can be interrogated by individual users that seek to carry out a transaction through online banking. Individual users that interact via this route do affect the deep web and the bank's underlying databases informationally while the entire deep web of the bank and its datasets remain hidden. Accumulation of data in the deep web along with the complexity that it engenders generate the need for further information processing via profiling, data mining or other techniques. These, in turn, are deployed for marketing, monitoring accounts for fraud or money laundering or other reasons and can structurally change the deep web itself, for example, through the implementation of new financial products. These new products also have to be accounted for in terms of information and become part of the surface web otherwise there would be no interconnection with the users.

It should be clear by now that the processes that participate within such a structural coupling between the surface web and the deep web are subtle and require further consideration. The self-referential character of information growth manifests itself through a multitude of complex and sometimes elusive processes, underpinned by different modes of interactions between the users and the information infrastructures within which they take place. Patterns of growth and modes of interaction reinforce one another. In this Appendix we focus on a mode of interaction that has considerably expanded information growth and will arguably continue to do so: the internet.

The purpose of this Appendix is to give some approximate indicators on some of these processes. We do not comment on the methodological assumptions that have underpinned the research through which these statistics have been generated. For these, the original authors are responsible. All original sources are acknowledged accordingly and a short commentary is provided in relation to each example.

Figure A.2   Increase of Surface Web and Deep Web

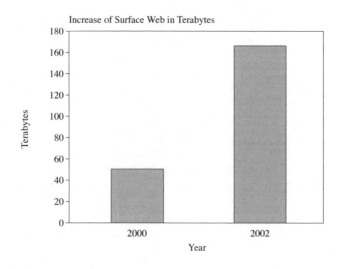

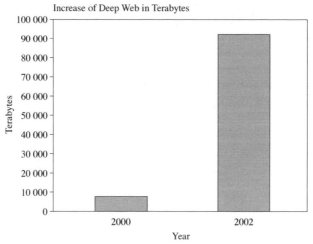

Source: http://www.sims.berkeley.edu/research/projects/how-much-info/
index.htm

Note: These graphs indicate the phenomenal estimated growth of both the
surface web as well as the deep web. According to the latest estimation of 2002,
the deep web is 91 850 terabytes. Taken that the entire print collections of the
US Library of Congress are estimated to be 10 terabytes one can begin to imagine the estimated extent of the deep web.

Figure A.3 Growth in Number of Internet Users

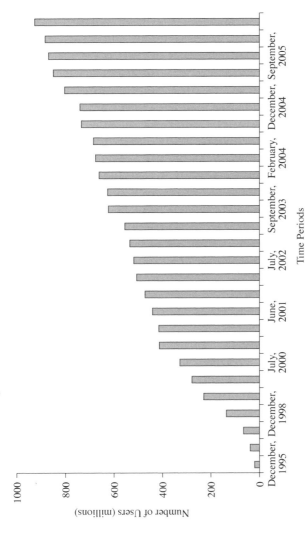

Source: http://www.internetworldstats.com/emarketing.htm

Note: From 16 million in December 1995 internet use has reached more than 1 billion users according to an estimation done in December 2005. The data in the source indicated comes from four different sources according to different time periods (after April 2000 however all statistics come from *Internet World Stats* as an information source). Despite the differences that could exist in underlying methodologies, the trend of growth in the number of internet users is clear.

Figure A.4   Growth of Internet Users as Percentage of World Population

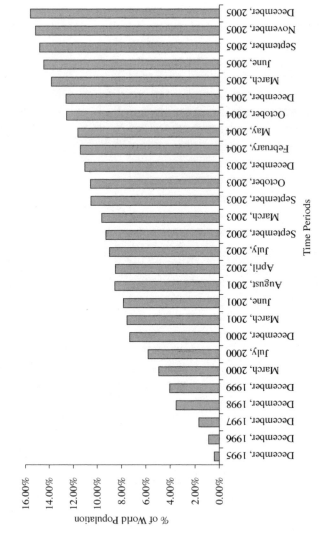

Source: http://www.internetworldstats.com/emarketing.htm

Note: It is worth pointing out that despite the phenomenal increase in numbers, it becomes evident by looking at the y-axis (% of the world population) that a little less than 16 per cent of the world's population approximately is using the internet. Clearly, the scope for further growth is considerable while the pace of growth is itself contingent upon several other factors.

Figure A.5   Percentage of Internet Usage Growth for 2000–2005

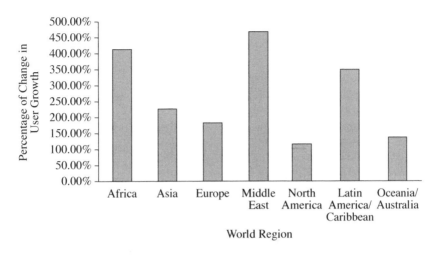

Source: http://www.internetworldstats.com

Note: Africa, the Middle East and Latin America are experiencing the highest growth but these regions still have a long way to go to bridge the digital divide. This is meant to be indicative of the difference in the growth rate and by no means depicts the intricacies of the digital divide, which is measurable with a variety of methodologies.

Figure A.6   Increase in Total Number of Internet Sites

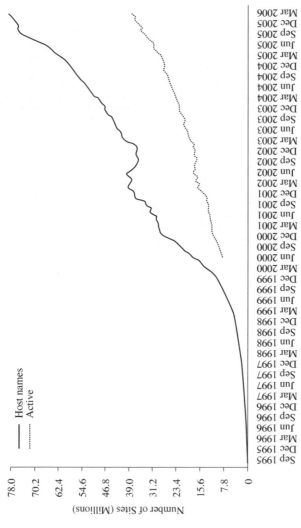

Source: http://news.netcraft.com/archives/web_server_survey.html

Note: A domain can be defined as a unique name that identifies an internet source (for example bbc.co.uk). What is surprising in the graph produced by Netcraft is the difference between the number of host names and those host names that are actually active. Such a difference indicates that a large number of host names are registered without actually being used (reasons for this are domain investing related to speculative buying for potentially reselling the host name). Despite such an important difference it becomes clear that both trends are exhibiting clear growth.

Figure A.7   Email Messaging Growth

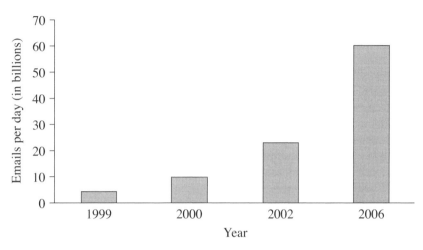

Source: http://www.sims.berkeley.edu/research/projects/how-much-info-2003/internet.htm

Note: This graph is based on data from the quoted source. However the primary source remains the study by the International Data Corporation. In 2003 the number of emails exchanged per day was around 30 billion. The projection for 2006 brought the number up to 60 billion emails per day. Further statistics of this type can be found at the web address given under source.

Figure A.8   An Example of Email Statistics

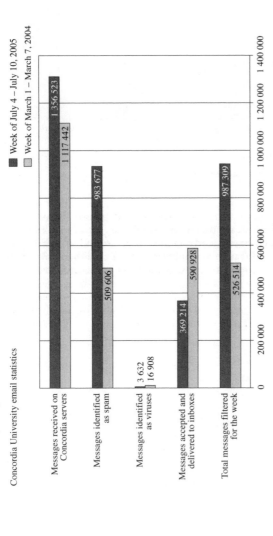

Concordia University email statistics

■ Week of July 4 – July 10, 2005
□ Week of March 1 – March 7, 2004

Source: http://iits.concordia.ca/statistics/email/

Note: With the growth of email exchange, the indiscriminate and unsolicited email messages that are being sent for various reasons (predominantly commercial advertising) have also considerably increased. The International Data Corporation[5] estimates that nearly half of the email messages being sent are spam. This example comes from the University of Concordia, where such a trend is clearly demonstrated. Such a considerable volume of unsolicited email messages does however impact on the broader information infrastructure in ways that need to be further researched.

5.   http://www.idc.com

Figure A.9   Dead Links in Search Engines

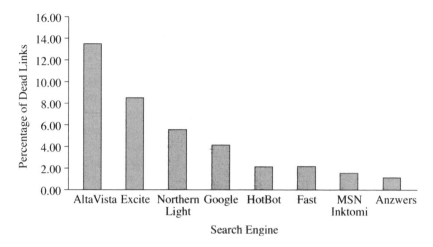

Source: http://www.searchengineshowdown.com

Note: Search engines play an important role in internet life as they facilitate requests for searching a complex information network such as the internet. The data used to produce the graph are based on a small survey that took place in the year 2000. Many things have clearly changed since (and search engines have considerably improved) but it is important to see that there are always differences between search engines and how they categorize information on their databases to facilitate the searches that a user will carry out. Even though that does not *per se* indicate information growth, it gives a glimpse of the underlying complexity (hyperlinks that remain searchable in search engines but that don't actually point to an existing web page).

Figure A.10 Differences in Search Engines

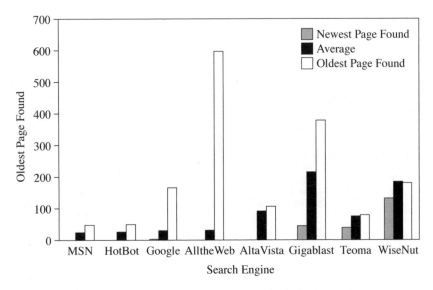

Source: http://www.searchengineshowdown.com/statistics/freshness.shtml

Note: Information indexed by databases has a time lag from what is actually going on in the internet. This graph gives the results of a small survey carried out in 2003. Not without reason, these statistics were originally labelled 'Freshness Statistics' and some of the key points were that the majority of the databases were about a month old while some pages may not have been re-indexed for a longer period of time than that. Despite the actual numbers that some might debate, the useful point to be made here is that there are bound to be differences between different search engines (due to different algorithmic representations and indexing methods) and that the 'freshness' of information categorized by databases is contingent upon their own algorithmic representations and deviates from the actual information generated online.

Figure A.11   The Phenomenon of Blogging

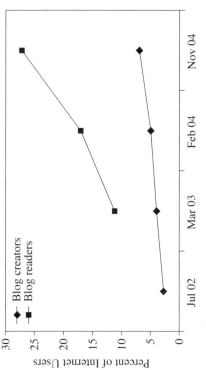

Source: www.technorati.com

Note: Blogging was introduced a few years ago and is now considered to be one of the most upcoming sources contributing to the growth of information. Blogging allows users to publish their thoughts, activities and so on, in the form of a website. The number of users active in blogging has dramatically increased over the past years and according to the estimations by Technorati[6] it is doubling every five months. Part of the reason for such an increase can be attributed to the widely available and simple tools that allow users to create their own blog without any knowledge of html or programming.

6.   A company that is tracking blogs.

Figure A.12   The Growth of the Blogosphere

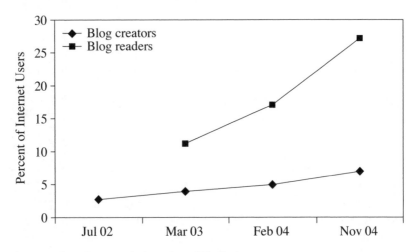

Source: Pew Internet & American Life Project

Note: Despite such an important rate of growth in blogging, it becomes evident from the research carried out by the Pew Internet & American Life Project that a little more than 6 per cent of internet users are active in blogging (latest data on this project was for November 2004 but that number has considerably increased if we follow the pattern of growth from Technorati – see Figure A.11). Perhaps even more interesting is the growth in the percentage of internet users that actively seek information from blogs instead of more traditional sources (such as news portals).

References

Abbott, A. (1988) *The Systems of Professions: An Essay on the Division of Expert Labor.* Chicago: The University of Chicago Press.

Adorno, T. and Horkheimer, M. (1972) *The Dialectic of Enlightenment.* London: Verso. Originally published in German in 1937.

Ahuja, M. K. and Carley, M. K. (1999) 'Network Structure in Virtual Organizations', *Organization Science*, 10/6: 741–57.

Aksoy, A. and Robins, K. (1992) 'Hollywood for the 21st Century: Global Competition for Critical Mass in Image Markets', *Cambridge Journal of Economics*, 16/1: 1–22.

Aldrich, H. (1979) *Organizations and Environments.* Englewood-Cliffs, NJ: Prentice Hall.

Archer, M. S. (2002) 'Realism and the Problem of Agency', *Journal of Critical Realism*, 5/1: 11–20.

Arendt, H. (1958) *The Human Condition.* Chicago: The University of Chicago Press.

Armbruster, T. (2005) 'Bureaucracy and the Controversy between Interventionism and Non-Interventionism', in Du Gay, P. (ed.) *The Values of Bureaucracy.* Oxford: Oxford University Press.

Arnheim, R. (1971) *Entropy and Art: An Essay on Disorder and Order.* Berkeley: University of California Press.

Arrow, K. J. (1974) *The Limits of Organization.* New York: Norton.

Arthur, W. B. (1988) 'Self-Reinforcing Mechanisms in Economics', in Anderson, P., Arrow, K. J. and Pines, D. (eds) *The Economy as an Evolving Complex System*, Vol. 5. Reading, MA: Addison Wesley.

Arthur, W. B. (1994) *Increasing Returns and Path Dependence in the Economy.* Ann Arbor: The University of Michigan Press.

Baecker, D. (2006) 'The Form of the Firm', *Organization*, 13/1: 109–42.

Barley, S. R. and Kunda, G. (2004) *Gurus, Hired Guns, and Warm Bodies: Itinerant Experts in a Knowledge Economy.* Princeton, NJ: Princeton University Press.

Barry, A. (2001) *Political Machines: Governing a Technological Society*. London: The Athlone Press.

Barthes, R. (1967) *Elements of Semiology*. New York: Noonday.

Bateson, G. (1972) *Steps to an Ecology of Mind*. New York: Ballantine.

Baudrillard, J. (1983) 'The Ecstasy of Communication', in Foster, H. (ed.) *The Anti-Aesthetic: Essays in Postmodern Culture*. Port Townsend: Bay Press.

Baudrillard, J. (1988) *Selected Writings*. Stanford: Stanford University Press.

Bauman, Z. (1992) *Intimations of Postmodernity*. London: Routledge.

Bauman, Z. (2000) *Liquid Modernity*. Cambridge: Polity.

Beck, U. (1992) *Risk Society: Towards a New Modernity*. London: Sage.

Beck, U. (2000) *The Brave New World of Work*. Cambridge: Polity.

Beck, U., Lash, S. and Giddens, A. (1996) *Reflexive Modernization*. Cambridge: Polity.

Becker, G. (1976) *The Economic Approach to Human Behavior*. Chicago: The University of Chicago Press.

Bell, D. (1976) *The Coming of the Post-Industrial Society*. New York: Basic Books.

Bendix, R. (1956) *Work and Authority in Industry*. New York: Wiley.

Benedikt, M. (1991) *Cyberspace: First Steps*. Cambridge, MA: The MIT Press.

Beniger, J. (1986) *The Control Revolution: Technological and Economic Origins of the Information Society*. Cambridge, MA: Harvard University Press.

Berger, P. L. and Luckmann, T. (1966) *The Social Construction of Reality: A Treatise in the Sociology of Knowledge*. London: Penguin.

Bijker, W. (2001) 'Understanding Technological Culture Through a Constructivist View of Science, Technology and Culture', in Cutcliffe, S. and Mitcham, C. (eds) *Visions of STS: Counterpoints in Science, Technology and Society Studies*. New York: State University of New York.

Bijker, W., Hughes, T. and Pinch, T. (eds) (1987) *The Social Construction of Technological Systems*. Cambridge, MA: The MIT Press.

Blau, P. M. (1955) *The Dynamics of Bureaucracy*. Chicago: The University of Chicago Press.

Blau, P. M. (1957) 'Formal Organizations: Dimensions of Analysis', *American Journal of Sociology*, 63: 58–69.

Bloomfield, B. and Vurdubakis, T. (2001) 'The Vision Thing: Construction of Time and Technology in Management Advice', in Clark, T. and Fincham, R. (eds) *Critical Consulting: Perspectives on the Management Advice Industry*. Oxford: Blackwell.

Bolter, J. D. (1991) *The Writing Space: The Computer, Hypertext and the History of Writing*. Hillsdale: Lea.

Bolter, J. D. and Grusin, R. (2000) *Remediation: Understanding New Media*. Cambridge, MA: The MIT Press.

Borgmann, A. (1984) *Technology and the Character of Contemporary Life: A Philosophical Inquiry.* Chicago: The University of Chicago Press.

Borgmann, A. (1999) *Holding On to Reality: The Nature of Information at the Turn of the Millennium*. Chicago: The University of Chicago Press.

Bowker, G. and Star, S. L. (1999) *Sorting Things Out: Classification and its Consequences*. Cambridge, MA: The MIT Press.

Boyden, M. (2003) 'The Rhetoric of Forgetting: Elena Esposito on Social Memory', *Image and Narrative*, 6, Medium Theory, www.imageandnarrative.be/mediumtheory/michaelboyden.htm

Braverman, H. (1974) *Labour and Monopoly Capital*. New York: The Monthly Review Press.

Brown, J. S. and Duguid, P. (2000) *The Social Life of Information*. Boston, MA: Harvard Business School Press.

Burns, T. and Stalker, G. (1961) *The Management of Innovation*. London: Tavistock.

Burt, R. S. (1982) *Towards a Structural Theory of Action: Network Models of Social Structure, Perception and Action*. New York: Academic Press.

Carnoy, M. (2000) *Sustaining the New Economy: Work, Family and Community in the Information Age*. Cambridge, MA: Harvard University Press.

Carrier, J. G. and Miller, D. (1998) *Virtualism: A New Political Economy*. Oxford: Berg.

Casey, C. (1999) '"Come Join Our Family": Discipline and Integration in Corporate Organizational Culture', *Human Relations*, 52/2: 155–78.

Casey, C. (2004) 'Bureaucracy Re-enchanted? Spirit, Experts and Authority in Organizations', *Organization*, 11/1: 59–79.

Casirrer, E. (1955) *The Philosophy of Symbolic Forms*, 3 Vols. New Haven: Yale University Press.

Castells, M. (1996) *The Rise of Network Society*. Oxford: Blackwell.

Castells, M. (2000) 'Materials for an Explanatory Theory of Network Society', *British Journal of Sociology*, 51/1: 5–24.

Castells, M. (2001) *The Internet Galaxy*. Oxford: Oxford University Press.

Castells, M. (2002) 'The Internet and the Network Society', in Wellman, B. and Haythornthwaite, C. (eds) *The Internet in Everyday Life*. Oxford: Blackwell.

Castoriadis, C. (1985) *The Bureaucratic Society*, 2 vols (in Greek). Athens: Ypsilon.

Castoriadis, C. (1987) *The Imaginary Institution of Society*. Stanford: Stanford University Press.

Chandler, A. D. (1962) *Strategy and Structure: Chapters in the History of the Industrial Enterprise*. Cambridge, MA: The MIT Press.

Chandler, A. D. (1977) *The Visible Hand: The Managerial Revolution in American Business*. Cambridge, MA: Harvard University Press.

Chandler, A. D. and Cortada, J. W. (2000) *A Nation Transformed by Information*. Oxford: Oxford University Press.

Chapman, R. A. (ed.) (2000) *Ethics in Public Service for the New Millennium*. Aldershot: Ashgate.

Ciborra, C. (1993) *Teams, Markets and Systems*. Cambridge: Cambridge University Press.

Ciborra, C. (1997) 'The Platform Organization: Recombining Strategies, Structures and Surprises', *Organization Science*, 7/2: 103–17.

Ciborra, C. (ed.) (2000) *From Control to Drift: The Dynamics of Corporate Information Infrastructures*. Oxford: Oxford University Press.

Ciborra, C. (2002) *The Labyrinths of Information*. Oxford: Oxford University Press.

Ciborra, C. (2006) 'Imbrications of Representations: Risk and Digital Technologies', *Journal of Management Studies*, 43/6: 1339–56.

Ciborra, C. and Lanzara, G. F. (1994) 'Formative Contexts and Information Technology', *Accounting, Management and Information Technologies*, 4: 611–26.

Cilliers, P. (2001) 'Boundaries, Hierarchies and Networks in Complex Systems', *International Journal of Innovation and Management*, 5/2: 195–27.

Clarke, J. (2005) 'Performing for the Public: Doubt, Desire, and the Evaluation of Public Services', in Du Gay, P. (ed.) *The Values of Bureaucracy*. Oxford: Oxford University Press.

Clarke, J. and Newman, J. (1997) *The Managerial State: Power, Politics and Ideology in the Remaking of Social Welfare*. London: Sage.

Clegg, S. (1994) 'Weber and Foucault: Social Theory for the Study of Organizations', *Organization* 1/1: 149–78.

Cline-Cohen, P. (1982) *A Calculating People: The Spread of Numeracy in Early America*. Chicago: The University of Chicago Press.

Coase, R. (1937) 'The Nature of the Firm', *Economica* 4: 386–405.

Cook, K. S. and Whitemeyer, J. M. (1992) 'Two Approaches to Social Structure: Exchange Theory and Network Analysis', *Annual Review of Sociology*, 18: 109–27.

Cooper, R. (1986) 'Organization/Disorganization', *Social Science Information*, 22/5: 299–335.

Cooper, R. (1989) 'The Visibility of Social Systems', in Jackson, M. C., Keys, P. and Cropper, S. A. (eds) *Operational Research and the Social Sciences*. New York: Plenum Press.

Cooper, R. (1991) 'Formal Organization as Representation: Remote Control, Displacement, Abbreviation', in Reed, M. and Hughes, M. (eds) *Rethinking Organization: New Directions in Organizational Analysis*. London: Sage.

Cooper, R. (2005) 'Relationality', *Organization Studies*, 26/11: 1689–710.

Cooper, R. and Kallinikos, J. (eds) (1996) 'Writing, Rationality and Organization', *Scandinavian Journal of Management*, 12/1, Special Issue.

Courpasson, D. and Reed, M. (eds) (2004) 'Special Issue on Bureaucracy in the Age of Enterprise', *Organization*, 11/1.

Davidow, W. H. and Malone, T. W. (1992) *The Virtual Corporation*. New York: Harper.

Deleuze, G. (1995) 'Postscript in Control Societies', in Deleuze, G., *Negotiations*, New York: Columbia University Press.

Derrida, J. (1978) *Writing and Difference*. Routledge: London.

DeSanctis, G. and Monge, P. (1999) 'Introduction to the Special Issue: Communication Processes for Virtual Organizations', *Organization Science*, 10/6: 693–703.

Devlin, K. (2001) *Infosense: Turning Information into Knowledge*. New York: Freeman and Company.

DiMaggio, P. J. (ed.) (2001) *The Twenty-First Century Firm*. Princeton: Princeton University Press.

DiMaggio, P. J., Hargittai, E., Russell Newman, W. and Robinson, J. P. (2001) 'Social Implications of the Internet', *Annual Review of Sociology*, 27: 307–36.

Douglas, M. (1986) *How Institutions Think*. Syracuse: Syracuse University Press.

Dreyfus, H. l. (2001) *On the Internet*. London: Routledge.

Dreyfus, H. I. and Dreyfus, S. E. (1986) *Mind over Machine*. New York: Free Press.

Du Gay, P. (1994) 'Colossal Immodesties and Hopeful Monsters', *Organization*, 1/1: 125–48.

Du Gay, P. (2000) *In Praise of Bureaucracy: Weber, Organization, Ethics*. London: Sage.

Du Gay, P. (ed.) (2005) *The Values of Bureaucracy*. Oxford: Oxford University Press.

Dumont, L. (1970) *Homo Hierarchicus: The Caste System and its Implications*. London: Weidenfeld and Nicolson.

Eccles, R. J. (1981) 'The Quasi Firm in the Construction Industry', *Journal of Economic Behavior and Organizations*, 2: 335–57.

Eco, U. (1976) *A Theory of Semiotics*. Bloomington: Indiana University Press.

Eisenstein, E. (1979) *The Printing Press as an Agent of Change: Communications and Cultural Transformations in Early-Modern Europe*, 2 Vols. Cambridge: Cambridge University Press.

Ekbia, H. R. and Kling, R. (2005) 'Network Organizations: Symmetric Cooperation or Multivalent Negotiation?', *Information Society*, 21: 155–68.

Ellul, J. (1964) *Technological Society*. New York: Vintage.

Esposito, E. (1996) 'Observing Interpretation: A Sociological View of Hermeneutics', *MLN*, 111: 593–619.

Esposito, E. (2003) 'The Arts of Contingency', *Critical Inquiry*, www.uchicago.edu/research/jnl-crit-inq/features/arts statements/arts.esposito.htm

Etzioni, A. (2000) *The Third Way to a Good Society*. London: Demos.

Evans, J. A., Kunda, G. and Barley, S. R. (2004) 'Beach Time, Bridge Time and Billable Hours: The Temporal Structure of Technical Consulting', *Administrative Science Quarterly*, 49/1: 1–38.

Fleck, J. (1994) 'Learning by Trying: The Implementation of Configurational Technology', *Research Policy*, 23: 737–652.

Fligstein, N. (1990) *The Transformation of Corporate Control*. Cambridge, MA: Harvard University Press.

Fligstein, N. (2001) *The Architecture of Markets*. Princeton: Princeton University Press.

Flusser, V. (2000) *The Shape of Things: A Philosophy of Design*. London: Reaktion Books.

Flusser, V (2003) *Die Schrift: hat Schreiben Zukunft?* Athens: Potamos (in Greek). Originally Published in German in 1987.

Forester, T. (ed.) (1989) *Computers in the Human Context*. Oxford: Blackwell.

Foucault, M. (1970) *The Order of Things*. London: Tavistock.

Foucault, M. (1977) *Discipline and Punish*. London: Penguin.

Foucault, M. (1980) *Power/Knowledge*. Edited by Gordon, C. New York: Pantheon.

Foucault, M. (1988) 'Technologies of the Self', in Martin, L. H., Gutman, H. and Hutton, P. H. (eds) *Technologies of the Self*. London: Tavistock.

Fountain, J. (2001) *Building the Virtual State*. Washington, D.C.: Brooking Institution Press.

Freidson, E. (2001) *Professionalism: The Third Logic*. Cambridge: Polity.

Fukuyama, F. (1997) *The End of Order*. London: Centre for Post-collectivist Studies.

Fulk, J. and DeSanctis, G. (1995) 'Electronic Communication and Changing Organization Forms', *Organization Science*, 6/4: 337–49.

Galbraith, J. (1973) *Organization Design*. Reading, MA: Addison-Wesley.

Garnham, N. (1990) *Capitalism and Communication*. London: Sage.

Garnham, N. (2004) 'Information Society as Theory and Ideology', in Webster, F. (ed.) *The Information Society Reader*. London: Routledge.

Gartner (2004) *Outsourcing Market: What the Future Holds*, www.gartner.com

Gellner, E. (1983) *Nations and Nationalism*. Oxford: Blackwell.

Gellner, E. (1996) *Conditions of Liberty: Civil Society and its Rivals*. London: Penguin.

Giddens, A. (1990) *The Consequences of Modernity*. Cambridge: Polity.

Giddens, A. (1991) *Modernity and Self-Identity*. Cambridge: Polity.

Giddens, A. (2000) *Runaway World*. London: Profile Books.

Goffman, E. (1961) *Asylums*. London: Penguin.

Goodman, N. (1976) *Languages of Art*. Indianapolis: Hackett.

Goodman, N. (1978) *Ways of Worldmaking*. Indianapolis: Hackett.

Goodman, N. (1984) *Of Mind and Other Matters*. Cambridge, MA: Harvard University Press.

Goody, J. (1977) *The Domestication of the Savage Mind*. Cambridge: Cambridge University Press.

Goody, J. (1986) *The Logic of Writing and the Organization of Society*. Cambridge: Cambridge University Press.

Grandori, A. and Soda, G. (1995) 'Inter-Firm Neworks: Antecedents, Mechanisms and Forms', *Organization Studies*, 16/2: 183–214.

Granovetter, M. (1985) 'Economic Action and Social Structure: The Problem of Embeddedness', *American Journal of Sociology*, 91/3: 481–510.

Greenfield, H. (1996) *Manpower and the Growth of Producer Services*. New York: Columbia University Press.

Habermas, J. (1987) *The Philosophical Discourse of Modernity*. Cambridge, MA: The MIT Press.

Hacking, I. (1990) *The Taming of Chance*. Cambridge: Cambridge University Press.

Hacking, I. (1999) *The Social Construction of What?* Cambridge, MA: Harvard University Press.

Hage, J. and Aiken, M. (1969) 'Routine Technology, Social Structure and Organization *Goals*', *Administrative Science Quarterly*, 14: 366–76.

Hägg, I. and Johanson, J. (1982) *Foretag i Natverk*. Stockholm: Naringsliv och Samhalle.

Håkansson, H. (ed.) (1982) *International Marketing and Purchasing of Industrial Goods: An Interaction Approach*. Chichester: Wiley.

Hall, R. (1982) *Organizations: Structure and Processes*. Englewood Cliffs, NJ: Prentice Hall.

Hanseth, O. (2000) 'The Economics of Standards', in Ciborra, C. (ed.) *From Control to Drift: The Dynamics of Corporate Information Infrastructures*. Oxford: Oxford University Press.

Hanseth, O. (2004) 'Knowledge as Infrastructure', in Avgerou, C., Ciborra, C. and Land, F. (eds) *The Social Study of Information and Communication Technology*. Oxford: Oxford University Press.

Hanseth, O. and Braa, K. (2000) 'Who is in Control, Designers, Managers – or Technology?' in Ciborra, C. (ed.) *From Control to Drift: The Dynamics of Corporate Information Infrastructures*. Oxford: Oxford University Press.

Hanseth, O., Ciborra, C. and Braa, K. (2001) 'The Control

Devolution: ERP and the Side Effects of Globalization', *The Database for Advances in Information Systems*, 32/4: 34–46.

Harrison B. (1994) *Lean and Mean*. New York: Basic Books.

Harvey, D. (1989) *The Condition of Postmodernity*. Cambridge: Blackwell.

Harvey, D. (2005) *A Brief History of Neoliberalism*. Oxford: Oxford University Press.

Hasselbladh, H. and Kallinikos, J. (2000) 'The Process of Rationalization: A Critique and Re-appraisal of Neo-institutionalism in Organization Studies', *Organization Studies*, 21/4: 697–720.

Hayek, F. (1945) 'The Use of the Knowledge in Society', *American Economic Review*, 35/4: 519–30.

Hayek, F. (1960) *The Constitution of Liberty*. London: Routledge.

Hayles, K. (1999) *How We Became Posthuman: Virtual Bodies in Cybernetics, Literature and Informatics*. Chicago: The University of Chicago Press.

Hayles, K. (2005) 'Computing the Human', *Theory, Culture and Society*, 22/1: 131–51.

Heckscher, C. and Donnellon, A. (eds) (1994) *The Post-Bureaucratic Organization*. London: Sage.

Heidegger, M. (1977) *The Question Concerning Technology and Other Essays*. New York: Harper.

Heller, A. (1999) *A Theory of Modernity*. Oxford: Blackwell.

Hinds, P. and Mortensen, M. (2005) 'Understanding Conflict in Geographically Distributed Teams: The Moderating Effects of Shared Identity, Shared Context, and Spontaneous Communication', *Organization Science*, 16/3: 290–307.

Hirsch, P. M. (2000) 'Cultural Industries Revisited', *Organization Science*, 11/3: 356–61.

Hirschman, A. (1977) *The Passions and the Interests*. Princeton, NJ: Princeton University Press.

Hodgson, D. F. (2004) 'Project Work: The Legacy of Bureaucratic Control in the Post-Bureaucratic Organization', *Organization*, 11/1: 81–100.

Hoskin, K. W. and Macve, R. H. (1986) 'Accounting and the Examination: A Genealogy of Disciplinary Power', *Accounting, Organizations and Society*, 11/2: 105–36.

Hughes, T. (2004) *Human-Built World: How to Think About Technology and Culture*. Chicago: The University of Chicago Press.

Hylland-Eriksen, T. (2001) *The Tyranny of the Moment: Fast and Slow Time in the Information Age*. London: Pluto Press.

Iannacci, F. (2005) *The Social Epistemology of Open Source Software Development: The Linux Case Study.* PhD Thesis, London: Department of Information Systems, London School of Economics and Political Science.

Introna, L. (1997) *Management, Information and Power.* London: Macmillan.

Introna, L. and Nissenbaum, H. (2000) 'The Politics of Search Engines', *Information Society*, 16/3: 169–85.

Jepperson, R. L. (1991) 'Institutions, Institutional Effects and Institutionalism', in Powell, W. W. and P. J. DiMaggio (eds) *The New Institutionalism in Organizational Analysis.* Chicago: The University of Chicago Press.

Jepperson, R. L. and Meyer, J. (1991) 'The Public Order and the Construction of Formal Organizations', in Powell, W. W. and P. J. DiMaggio (eds) *The New Institutionalism in Organizational Analysis.* Chicago: The University of Chicago Press.

Jessop, B. (2002) *The Future of the Capitalist State.* Cambridge: Polity.

Kallinikos, J. (1993) 'Identity, Recursiveness and Change: Semiotics and Beyond', in Ahonen, P. (ed.) *Tracing the Semiotic Boundaries of Politics.* Berlin: de Gruyter.

Kallinikos, J. (1995) 'Cognitive Foundations of Economic Institutions: Markets, Organizations and Networks Revisited', *Scandinavian Journal of Management*, 11/2: 119–37.

Kallinikos, J. (1996) *Technology and Society: Interdisciplinary Studies in Formal Organization.* Munich: Accedo.

Kallinikos, J. (1998a) 'Organized Complexity: Posthumanist Remarks on the Technologizing of Intelligence', *Organization*, 5/3: 371–96.

Kallinikos, J. (1998b) 'Utilities, Toys and Make-Believe: Remarks on the Instrumental Experience', in Chia, R. (ed.) *In the Realm of Organization: Essays for Robert Cooper.* London: Routledge.

Kallinikos, J. (1999) 'Computer-based Technology and the Constitution of Work: A Study on the Cognitive Foundations of Work', *Accounting, Management and Information Technologies*, 9/4: 261–91.

Kallinikos, J. (2001) *In the Age of Flexibility: Managing Organizations and Technology.* Lund: Academia Adacta.

Kallinikos, J. (2002) 'Re-opening the Black Box of Technology: Artifacts and Human Agency', in Galliers, R. and Markus, L. (eds) *23rd International Conference on Information Systems*, Barcelona, 14–16 December, pp. 287–94.

Kallinikos, J. (2003) 'Work, Employment and Organization Forms: An Anatomy of Fragmentation', *Organization Studies*, 24/4: 595–618.

Kallinikos, J. (2004a) 'The Social Foundations of the Bureaucratic Order', *Organization*, 11/1: 13–36.

Kallinikos, J. (2004b) 'Deconstructing Information Packages: Organizational and Behavioural Implications of ERP Systems', *Information Technology and People*, 17/1: 8–30.

Kallinikos, J. (2004c) 'Farewell to Constructivism: Technology and Context-Embedded Action', in Avgerou, C., Ciborra, C. and Land, F. (eds) *The Social Study of Information and Communication Technology*. Oxford: Oxford University Press.

Kallinikos, J. (2005) 'The Order of Technology: Complexity and Control in a Connected World', *Information and Organization*, 15/3: 185–202.

Kallinikos, J. (2006a) 'Information out of Information: On the Self-Referential Dynamics of Information Growth', *Information Technology and People*, 19/1: 98–115.

Kallinikos, J. (2006b) 'The Institution of Bureaucracy: Administration, Pluralism, Democracy', *Economy and Society*, 35/4: 611–27.

Kelly, J. E. (1998) *Rethinking Industrial Relations. Mobilization, Collectivism and Long Waves*. London: Routledge.

Kittler, F. (1996) *The History of Communication Media*, http://www.ctheory.net/articles.aspx?id=45.

Kittler, F. (1997) *Literature, Media, Information Systems*. Amsterdam: OPA.

Klaus, H. (2004) *Elements of a Hermeneutics of Knowledge in Government: The Coalition of Public Sector Reform and Enterprise Resource Planning*. PhD Thesis. Brisbane: Queensland University of Technology.

Klein, H. K. and Kleinman, D. L. (2002) 'The Social Construction of Technology: Structural Considerations', *Science, Technology and Human Values*, 27/1: 28–52.

Kling, R. (ed.) (1996) *Computerization and Controversy: Value Conflicts and Social Choices*. San Diego: Morgan Kauffman, Second Edition.

Knorr-Cetina, K. and Bruegger, U. (2002) 'Global Microstructures: The Virtual Societies of Financial Markets', *American Journal of Sociology*, 107/4: 905–50.

Kraakman, R. (2001) 'The Durability of the Corporate Form', in DiMaggio, P. J. (ed.) *The Twenty-First Century Firm*. Princeton: Princeton University Press.

190   *The Consequences of Information*

Kumar, K. (1995) *From Post-Industrial to Post-Modern Society*. Oxford: Blackwell.

Kunda, G. (1992) *Engineering Culture: Control and Commitment in a High-Tech Corporation*. Philadelphia: Temple University Press.

Lackoff, G. (1995) 'Body, Brain and Communication', in Brook, J. and Boal, I. A. (eds) *Resisting the Virtual Life*. San Francisco: City Lights.

Lampel, J. and Mintzberg, H. (1996) 'Customizing Customization', *Sloan Management Review*, Fall: 21–30.

Lash, S. (2001) 'Technological Forms of Life', *Theory, Culture and Society*, 18/1: 105–20.

Lash, S. (2002) *Critique of Information*. London: Sage.

Law, J. (ed.) (1991) *A Sociology of Monsters: Essays on Power, Technology and Domination*. London: Routledge.

Leach, E. (1976) *Culture and Communication: The Logic by which Symbols are Connected*. Cambridge: Cambridge University Press.

LeGrand, J. and W. Bartlett (eds) (1993) *Quasi-Markets and Social Policy*. London: Macmillan.

Lessig, L. (2002) *The Future of Ideas: The Fate of Commons in a Connected World*. New York: Vintage.

Lilley, S., Lightfoot, G. and Amaral, P. (2004) *Representing Organization*. Oxford: Oxford University Press.

Luckmann, T. (2005) *On the Communicative Construction of Reality*, http://is2.lse.ac.uk/Events/LuckmannLecture.pdf.

Luhmann, N. (1982) *The Differentiation of Society*. New York: Columbia University Press.

Luhmann, N. (1993) *Risk: A Sociological Theory*. Berlin: De Gruyter.

Luhmann, N. (1995) *Social Systems*. Stanford: Stanford University Press.

Luhmann, N. (1996) 'Complexity, Structural Contingency and Value Conflicts', in Heelas, P., Lash, S. and Morris, P. (eds) *Detraditionalization*. Oxford: Blackwell.

Luhmann, N. (1998) *Observations on Modernity*. Stanford, CA: Stanford University Press.

Luhmann, N. (2002) *Theories of Distinction*. Stanford, CA: Stanford University Press.

Lyman, P., Varian, H. R. and Associates (2003) *How Much Information*, http://www.sims.berkeley.edu/research/projects/how-much-info-2003/index.htm

Lyotard, J.-F. (1984) *The Postmodern Condition*. Manchester: Manchester University Press.

Lyotard, J.-F. (1991) *The Inhuman*. Cambridge: Polity Press.

Malone, T. W. (2004) *The Future of Work*, Boston: Harvard Business School Press.

Malone, T. W. and Laubacher, R. (1998) 'The Dawn of the E-Lance Economy', *Harvard Business Review*, September–October: 145–52.

Mangham, I. L. (1995) 'MacIntyre and the Manager', *Organization*, 2/2: 181–204.

Maravelias, C. (2003) 'Post-Bureaucracy: Control Through Professional Freedom', *Journal of Organizational Change Management*, 16/5: 547–66.

March, J. G. (1988) *Decisions in Organizations*. New York: Free Press.

March, J. G. (1994) *A Premier on Decision Making*. New York: Free Press.

March, J. G. and Olsen, J. P. (1976) *Ambiguity and Choice in Organizations*. Bergen: Universitetsforlaget.

March, J. G. and Olsen, J. P. (1989) *Rediscovering Institutions*. New York: Free Press.

March, J. G. and Simon, H. A. (1993) *Organizations*. New York: Wiley, Second Edition, originally published in 1958.

Marchington, M., Grimshaw, D., Rubery, J. and Willmott, H. (2005) *Fragmenting Work: Blurring Organizational Boundaries and Disordering Hierarchies*. Oxford: Oxford University Press.

Marcuse, H. (1955) *Eros and Civilization*. Boston: Beacon Press.

Marx, K. (1954 and 1956) *The Capital*. Two Volumes. Moscow: Progress Publishers. Originally Published in 1865 and 1867 respectively.

McGregor, D. (1960) *The Human Side of the Enterprise*. New York: McGraw Hill.

Meyer, J. (1994) 'Rationalized Environments', in Scott, R. W. and Meyer, J. (eds) *Institutional Environments and Organizations*. London: Sage.

Miller, D. (ed.) (1995) *Acknowledging Consumption*. London: Routledge.

Mintzberg, H. (1979) *The Structuring of Organizations*. Englewood Cliffs, NJ: Prentice Hall.

Mintzberg, H. (1983) *Structures in Fives*. Englewood Cliffs, NJ: Prentice Hall.

Misa, T., Brey, P. and Feenberg, A. (eds) (2003) *Modernity and Technology*. Cambridge. MA: The MIT Press.

Morgan, G. (1986) *Images of Organization*. London: Sage.

Mowshowitz, A. (2002) *Virtual Organization: Toward a Theory of Societal Transformation Stimulated by Information Technology*. Westport, CT: Quorum Books.

Mumford, L. (1934) *Technics and Civilization*. London: Harvest/HBJ.

Mumford, L. (1952) *Arts and Technics*. New York: Columbia University Press.

Mumford, L. (1970) *The Myth of the Machine: The Pentagon of Power*. 2 Vols. New York: Columbia University Press.

Murray, G., Belanger, J., Giles, A. and Lapointe, P.-A. (2002) *Work and Employment Relations in the High-Performance Workplace*. London: Continuum.

Neisser, U. (1976) *Cognition and Reality: Principles and Implications of Cognitive Psychology*. San Francisco: Freeman.

Newman, J. (2005) 'Bending Bureaucracy: Leadership and Multi-Level Governance', in Du Gay, P. (ed.) *The Values of Bureaucracy*. Oxford: Oxford University Press.

Noble, D. (1984) *Forces of Production: A Social History of Industrial Automation*. New York: Alfred A. Knopf.

Nohria, N. and Buckley, J. D. (1994) 'The Virtual Organization: Bureaucracy, Technology and the Implosion of Control', in Heckscher, C. and Donnellon, A. (eds) *The Post-Bureaucratic Organization: New Perspectives in Organizational Change*. London: Sage.

Nohria, N. and Eccles, R. (eds) (1992) *Networks and Organizations: Structure, Form and Action*. Cambridge, MA: Harvard Business Press.

North, D. (1981) *Structure and Change in Economic History*. London: Norton.

North, D. (1990) *Institutions, Institutional Change and Economic Performance*. Cambridge: Cambridge University Press.

Ong, W. (1982) *Orality and Literacy: The Technologizing of the Word*. London: Routledge.

Orlikowski, W. J. (1996) 'Evolving with Notes: Organizational Change around Groupware Technology', in Ciborra, C. (ed.) *Groupware and Teamwork: Invisible Aid or Technical Hindrance*. London: Wiley.

Orlikowski, W. J. (2000) 'Using Technology and Constituting Structures: A Practice Lens for Studying Technology in Organizations', *Organization Science*, 11/4: 404–28.

Orlikowski, W. J., Walsham, G., Jones, M. R. and DeGross, J. I. (eds) (1996) *Information Technology and Changes in Organizational Work*. London: Chapman & Hall.

Osborne, D. and Gaebler, T. (1992) *Reinventing Government: How the Entrepreneurial Spirit is Transforming the Public Sector*. Reading, MA: Addison-Wesley.

Osborne, T. (1994) 'Bureaucracy as Vocation: Governmentality and Administration in Nineteenth Century Britain', *Journal of Historical Sociology*, 7/3: 289–313.

Parsons, T. (1956a) 'Suggestions for a Sociological Approach to the Theory of Organizations I', *Administrative Science Quarterly*, 1/1: 63–86.

Parsons, T. (1956b) 'Suggestions for a Sociological Approach to the Theory of Organizations II', *Administrative Science Quarterly*, 1/2: 225–40.

Perrow, C. (1967) 'A Framework for the Comparative Analysis of Organizations', *American Sociological Review*, 32/2: 194–208.

Perrow, C. (1984) *Normal Accidents: Living with High Risk Technologies*. New York: Basic Books.

Perrow, C. (1986) *Complex Organizations: A Critical Essay*. New York: Random House, Third Edition.

Perrow, C. (2002) *Organizing America: Wealth, Power and the Origins of Corporate Capitalism*. Princeton: Princeton University Press.

Piore, M. and Sabel, C. (1984) *The Second Industrial Divide: Possibilities for Prosperity*. New York: Basic Books.

Postman, N. (1992) *Technopoly: The Surrender of Culture to Technology*. New York: Vintage.

Powell, W. W. (1990), 'Neither Market nor Hierarchy: Network Forms of Organization', in Staw, B. and Cummings, L. (eds) *Research in Organizational Behaviour*. Greenwich, CT: JAI.

Powell, W. W. (2001) 'The Capitalist Firm in the Twenty-First Century: Emerging Patterns in Western Enterprise', in DiMaggio, P. J. (ed.) *The Twenty-First Century Firm*. Princeton: Princeton University Press.

Powell, W. W. and DiMaggio, P. J. (eds) (1991) *The New Institutionalism in Organizational Analysis*. Chicago: Chicago University Press.

Pugh, D., Hickson, D., Hinings, C., Macdonald, K., Turner, C. and Lupton, T. (1963) 'A Conceptual Scheme for Organizational Analysis', *Administrative Science Quarterly*, 8: 289–315.

Pugh, D., Hickson, D., Hinings, C. and Turner, C. (1968)

'Dimensions of Organizational Structure', *Administrative Science Quarterly*, 13: 65–104.

Reed, M. (2005) 'Beyond the Iron Cage? Bureaucracy and Democracy in the Knowledge Economy and Society', in Du Gay, P. (ed.) *The Values of Bureaucracy*. Oxford: Oxford University Press.

Ricoeur, P. (1977) *The Rule of Metaphor: Multidisciplinary Studies in the Creation of Meaning in Language*. Toronto: Toronto University Press.

Rifkin, J. (1995) *The End of Work*. New York: Putnam.

Rifkin, J. (2000) *The Age of Access*. London: Penguin.

Rolland, K. H. and Monteiro, E. (2002) 'Balancing the Local and the Global in Infrastructural Information Systems', *Information Society*, 18: 87–100.

Rose, N. (1999) *Powers of Freedom: Reframing Political Thought*. Cambridge: Cambridge University Press.

Sassen, S. (2001) *The Global City*. Princeton: Princeton University Press.

Sassen, S. (2004) 'Towards a Sociology of Information Technology', in Avgerou, C., Ciborra, C. and Land, F. (eds) *The Social Study of Information and Communication Technology*. Oxford: Oxford University Press.

Schmidt, K. and Bannon, L. (1992) 'Taking CSCW Seriously: Supporting Articulation Work', *CSCW*, 1/1–2: 7–40.

Schofield, J. (2006) 'It's All in the Mix', *The Guardian*, Thursday, 2 February.

Scott, R. W. (1981) *Organizations: Rational, Natural and Open Systems*. Englewood Cliffs, NJ: Prentice Hall.

Scott, R. W. (1995) *Institutions and Organizations*. London: Sage.

Searle, J. (1995) *The Construction of Social Reality*. London: Penguin.

Sennett, R. (1992) *The Fall of Public Man*. New York: Norton.

Sennett, R. (2000) *The Corrosion of Character: The Personal Consequences of Work in the New Capitalism*. New York: Norton.

Sennett, R. (2006) *The Culture of New Capitalism*. New York: Yale University Press.

Seyer, D. (1991) *Capitalism and Modernity: An Excursus of Marx and Weber*. London: Routledge.

Shannon, C. and Weaver, W. (1949) *The Mathematical Theory of Communication*. Urbana: The University of Illinois Press.

Shiller, R. J. (2003) *The New Financial Order*. Princeton: Princeton University Press.

Simon, H. A. (1969) *The Sciences of the Artificial.* Cambridge, MA: The MIT Press.

Simon, H. A. (1977) *The New Science of Management Decision.* Englewood Cliffs, NJ: Prentice Hall.

Sinha, K. K. and Van de Ven, A. H. (2005) 'Designing Work Within and Between Organizations', *Organization Science*, 16/4: 389–408.

Sotto, R. (1991) *Man Without Knowledge: Actors and Spectators in Organizations.* Stockholm: Stockholm University Press.

Sproull, L. S. and Kiesler, S. B. (1991) *Connections: New Ways of Working in the Networked Organization.* Cambridge, MA: MIT Press.

Star, S.-L. and Ruhleder, K. (1994) 'Steps Towards an Ecology of Infrastructure', *CSCW*, 10: 253–64.

Steinmueller, E. W. (2002) 'Virtual Communities and the New Economy', in Mansell, R. (ed.) *Inside the Communication Revolution: Evolving Patterns of Social Interaction.* Oxford: Oxford University Press.

Storper, M. (1989) 'The Transition to Flexible Specialization in US Film Industry: External Economies, the Division of Labour, and the Crossing of Industrial Divides', *Cambridge Journal of Economics*, 13/2: 273–305.

Storper, M. (1993) 'Flexible Specialization in Hollywood: A Response to Aksoy and Robins', *Cambridge Journal of Economics*, 17/4: 479–84.

Suchman, L. (1996) 'Articulation Work', in Kling, R. (ed.) *Computerization and Controversy.* San Diego: Academic Press.

Thompson, J. D. (1967) *Organizations in Action.* New York: McGraw Hill.

Thompson, G. F. (2003) *Between Networks and Hierarchies: The Logic and Limits of Network Forms of Organization.* Oxford: Oxford University Press.

Thompson. G. F. (2004) 'Getting to Know the Knowledge Economy: ICTs, Networks and Governance', *Economy and Society*, 33/4: 562–81.

Thompson, P. and Alvesson, M. (2005) 'Bureaucracy at Work: Misunderstandings and Mixed Blessings', in Du Gay, P. (ed.) *The Values of Bureaucracy.* Oxford: Oxford University Press.

Tilly, C. (2001) 'Welcome to the Seventeenth Century', in DiMaggio, P. J. (ed.) *The Twenty-First Century Firm.* Princeton: Princeton University Press.

Townley, B. (1994) *Reframing Human Resource Management.* London: Sage.

Tsivacou, I. (1997) *With the Eye of the Observer: Description and Design of Social Organizations*. Athens: Themelio (in Greek).

Tsivacou, I. (2003) *Flexibility and Boundaries in Social Systems*. Athens: Nefeli (in Greek).

Tsoukas, H. (1996) 'The Firm as Distributed Knowledge System: A Constructionist Approach', *Strategic Management Journal*, 17: 11–25.

Vattimo, G. (1989) *The End of Modernity*. Cambridge: Polity Press.

Venkatesh, M. (2003) 'The Community Network Life Cycle: A Framework for Research and Action', *Information Society*, 19: 339–47.

Virilio, P. (2000) *The Information Bomb*. London: Verso.

Weber, M. (1947) *The Theory of Social and Economic Organization*. London: Free Press.

Weber, M. (1970) *From Max Weber*. London: Routledge. Edited by Gerth, H. & C. Wright Mills.

Weber, M. (1978) *Economy and Society*, 2 Vols. Berkeley: University of California Press. Edited by Roth, G. and Wittich, C.

Webster, F. (ed) (2002) *Theories of the Information Society*. London: Routledge.

Webster, F. (ed.) (2004) *The Information Society Reader*. London: Routledge.

Weick, K. E. (1979a) *The Social Psychology of Organizing*. Reading, MA: Addison Wesley.

Weick, K. E. (1979b) 'Cognitive Processes in Organizations', in Staw, B. M. (ed.) *Research in Organizational Behaviour*. London: JAI.

Wellman, B. (ed.) (1999) *Networks in the Global Village*. Boulder, CO: Westview Press.

Wellman, B. and Haythornthwaite, C. (2002) *The Internet in Everyday Life*. Oxford: Blackwell.

Wellman, B., Salaff, J., Dimitrova, D., Garton, I., Gulia, M. and Haythornthwaite, C. (1996) 'Computer Networks as Social Networks: Collaborative Work, Telework and Virtual Community', *Annual Review of Sociology*, 22: 213–38.

White, H. C. (1981) 'Where do Markets Come From?', *American Journal of Sociology*, 85: 517–47.

White, H. C. (2002) *Markets from Networks: Socioeconomic Models of Production*. Princeton, NJ: Princeton University Press.

Wigand, R., Picot, A. and Reichwald, R. (1997) *Information, Organization and Management*. New York: Wiley.

Williams, D. (2006) 'Can I Hear Me Now?' *Harvard Business Review*, February: 37–8.

Williamson, O. E. (1975) *Markets and Hierarchies*. New York: Free Press.

Williamson, O. E. (1981) 'The Economics of Organization: The Transaction Cost Approach', *American Journal of Sociology*, 87/3: 548–77.

Williamson, O. E. (1985) *The Economic Institutions of Capitalism*. New York: Basic Books.

Winner, L. (1977) *Autonomous Technology. Technics-out-of-Control as a Theme in Political Thought*. Cambridge, MA: The MIT Press.

Winner, L. (1986) *The Whale and the Reactor: A Search of Limits in the Age of High Technology*. Chicago: The University of Chicago Press.

Winner, L. (1993) 'Upon Opening the Black Box and Finding it Empty: Social Constructivism and the Philosophy of Technology', *Science, Technology and Human Values*, 18: 362–78.

Winter, S. J. and Taylor, S. L. (2001) 'The Role of Information Technology In the Transformation of Work: A Comparison of Post-Industrial, Industrial, and Proto-Industrial Organization', in Yates, J. and Van Maanen, J. (eds) *Information Technology and Organizational Transformation*. London: Sage.

Woolgar, S. (ed.) (2002) *Virtual Society: Technology, Cyberbole, Reality*. Oxford: Oxford University Press.

Yates, J. (1989) *Control through Communication: The Rising of System in American Management*. Baltimore: Johns Hopkins University Press.

Yates, J. and Van Maanen, J. (eds) (2001) *Information Technology and Organizational Transformation*. London: Sage.

Zuboff, S. (1988) *In the Age of the Smart Machine*. New York: Basic Books.

Zuboff, S. and Maxmin, J. (2003) *The Support Economy: How Corporations are Failing Individuals and the Next Episode of Capitalism*. London: Allen Lane.

Name Index

Subject Index

reversibility 143, 152
rights 113, 116, 120, 126, 138, 139, 161
risk 39, 40, 48, 59
role re-engineering 119, 145
rule-bound behaviour 7, 132, 142

second-order processing 57
selectivity 36, 143
self-referential information growth 98
semantic information 53
semantics 53, 77
sign tokens 35, 52, 61, 69
skill updatability 145
software engineering 37, 157
solidification 111, 139
specialization 13, 93, 97–9, 130, 131, 135, 148, 149
standardization 8, 23, 25–6, 27–8, 30, 34, 36–8, 61, 64–5, 69, 74, 93, 130, 131, 132, 148, 149, 150
stratification 135, 136, 147
structural configuration 9, 131
structural coupling 165, 167
structural differentiation 109–10, 160

structural principle 133, 136, 138, 139, 142
subcontracting 13, 92, 103, 106

tangibility 156, 158
task infrastructure 2, 14, 90, 95, 107, 109, 155, 156
technological paradigm 6, 23, 27, 30, 31, 89, 95
time and information 25, 26, 27, 49, 50, 54–7, 58, 70, 73, 78, 83, 97, 111, 112, 115, 164
total organizations 119, 136–9, 149
transferability 18, 29, 46, 93, 97, 160

universalism 135
updatability 71, 145
updating 50, 71–3, 75, 164

value of information 53–4, 70, 71, 72, 81
virtual organization 103–4, 145
virtual relations 143, 145

zones of interoperability 15, 38, 43–4, 46, 49, 159